One
Way
To
Write
YOUR
NOVEL

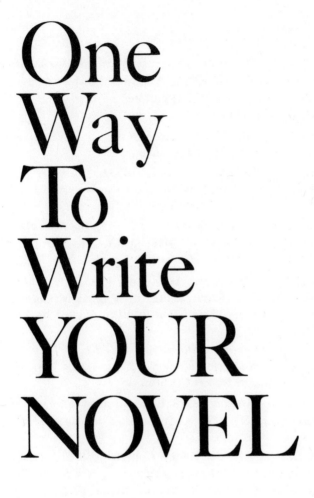

One Way To Write YOUR NOVEL

By Dick Winfield*

WRITER'S DIGEST, 22 E. 12TH ST., CINCINNATI, OHIO 45210

Acknowledgments

PN
3355
.W6

William Faulkner quotation from *Writers at Work, The Paris Review Interviews,* First Series, Edited by Malcolm Cowley. Copyright 1957-58 by *The Paris Review, Inc.* Reprinted by permission of The Viking Press, New York.

Richard Condon quotation from *Conversations,* by Roy Newquist, Copyright 1967 by Rand McNally & Company.

Alberto Moravia quotation from *Writers at Work, The Paris Review Interviews,* First Series, Edited by Malcolm Cowley. Reprinted by permission of The Viking Press, New York.

Georges Simenon quotation from *Writers at Work, The Paris Review Interviews,* First Series, Edited by Malcolm Cowley. Reprinted by permission of The Viking Press, New York.

John Fowles quotation (Copyright 1969, John Fowles) from *Afterwords: Novelists on Their Novels,* Edited by Thomas McCormack, Harper & Row, New York. Permission to quote granted by Julian Bach, Jr. Literary Agency.

Robert Crichton quotation from *Afterwords: Novelists on Their Novels,* Edited by Thomas McCormack, Harper & Row, New York. Permission to quote granted by Robert Crichton.

Passage from *Tales of Manhattan,* by Louis Auchincloss, Copyright 1967 by Louis Auchincloss. By permission of Houghton Mifflin Company, Boston.

Passage from *Hotel,* by Arthur Hailey, Copyright© 1965 by Arthur Hailey, Ltd., Published in hardcover by Doubleday & Co., Inc., New York. Bantam edition by Bantam Books, Inc., New York.

Passage from *The Agony and the Ecstasy,* by Irving Stone, Copyright© 1961 by Doubleday and Co., Inc. Signet edition by New American Library, New York.

Standard Book Number 911654-13-5

Library of Congress Catalog Card Number: 77-100316

Writer's Digest, 22 E. Twelfth Street, Cincinnati, Ohio 45210
Published 1969

Printed in the United States of America

Preface

As soon as rules are laid down for the writing of a novel, they will be brilliantly broken by the maverick nature of a born novelist. Yet, a writer does need to be aware of the workings of the forms he has chosen to handle if he is to be successful in bending them to his uses. He must know their properties quite as an architect must know what stresses a given span of concrete will bear. If he does not know, he will ask of them things they cannot accomplish and neglect to ask of them the utmost in achieving his purposes.

Because certain matters must be understood before any system for the production of a novel can be used effectively, some reminders are included in the Supplements to this book for those of us who have been too long away from a basic analysis of the novel form.

Contents

1 *Watch That First Step*   *1*

So you're going to write a novel? Welcome. Some tricks of the trade. Here is my way. To write your book will be fun. Finding the 26 hour day. Write efficiently. What it's all about. A step at a time. The only thing this piece of writing won't do is tuck you in bed. Remember, you're not alone.

2 *How to Write a Novel in 100 Days*   *7*

Where do novels come from? How to write in spite of anything. Relax, you don't have to write as much as you think. Broadcast your intentions. When is the best time to write? Write what you're in the mood for; we'll organize later. Keep on schedule. Just two pages a day. Plan ahead. Make every minute count. How to think out your writing while you do dishes or commute to work. How to use your weekends effectively. No holidays for novelists. If *I* can write this chapter, *you* can write a novel—dozens of them, in fact.

3 *Creating an Unforgettable Character*   *14*

Now let's get started. What your novel will be about. *You* can choose where to begin. Creating characters. How to fabricate a character from thin air in ten minutes. Aunt Tilly—you can't know too much about her. Aunt Tilly comes alive. What about using real people? The composite character. How to make Aunt Tilly seethe, burn, simmer, sizzle, smolder and much more. Use your thesaurus. How to describe Aunt Tilly with a sentence here, a word there. Keep her in character. Now create some more characters. Don't wait for inspiration to strike, get started now.

4 *It Takes Two to Dialogue*   *25*

How dialogue hooks the reader. Dialogue keeps the reader tuned in. Hilda and Herbert: dialogue presents two points of view. Someone on the reader's side. Dialogue makes the reader feel he's where the action is. Dialogue fills pages and breaks the monotony. Dialogue moves the story forward. How to make your dialogue sound real. Edit. Keep your dialogue efficient. How to develop an ear for dialogue. Dialects and the vernacular. Let your reader in on what your characters are talking about. Foreign language in a novel. Let your reader know who is speaking. "Said"—one of the nicest and hardest working words in your vocabulary. Be indiscreet discreetly.

5 *Where Does Your Novel Happen?*   *35*

Get that faraway look out of your eyes. Leave the frozen tundra to somebody else; leave Notre Dame to Quasimodo. Be practical; you *can* bring ordinary settings to life. How to turn the ordinary into art. The wonderful things only *you* know. Don't let your settings overpower the plot. Don't trust your memory; research your setting. How to do it—easily.

6 Description in Small Doses   42

One paragraph is better than a dozen. Hilda and Herbert and the specifications of a telephone booth. Don't describe what doesn't need describing. A few quick sentences can give your reader the idea. Contrast in description. Readers read over bromides. Be specific. A sentence should describe action or describe an object; it shouldn't do both. How to edit for strength.

7 Four Ways to Put Pizzazz in Your Novel   50

What makes your novel drag. Imagination is the key. Find a different way for your characters to accomplish the ordinary. Use contrasts. How to liven your plot. Counterpoint. How to add dimension to your novel. How to make your settings vivid. Season with foibles; tamper with time; add counter-melody.

8 Is Sex Necessary?   57

How much sex should your novel contain? A rousing novel need not arouse. Asterisks. You don't have to be explicit. Read some *good* erotic writing. Don't presume knowledge; mind your research. Why are sex scenes necessary? Sweet nothings: Dialogue in the sex scene. Teenage sex. Average, grown-up sex. The big difference between men and women. The love battle. Clinical detail only shocks. People in their birthday suits. Where do urchins come from? What *was* Peyton Place all about?

9 *Everyone Laughed When I Sat Down*   *64*
     at the Typewriter

Should you (ha ha) put humor in your novel? What kind of sense of humor do you have? Don't try to define humor. Natural humor is better than forced humor. Real life is funny enough. How to put humor in your setting. How to use words skillfully to inject humor. Don't forget about contrast. Inside jokes. Humor has no set pattern. You can't make jokes with a computer. Please yourself.

10 *Having Something to Say—and Letting*   *70*
     Your Characters Say It

Who and what you are shines through every page. Beware of authorial interjection. When you make your Great Point, make sure the reader doesn't see you coming. Be what you are, write what you must. Get the reader involved. Novels worth their salt do make points and have messages.

11 *The Way It Was—Exactly*   *76*

When we fix a moment in time, that moment is history; and history requires research. People remember dates. Checking facts. Research *can* be fun. How to research easily by checking old newspapers. Develop your own research method. Caution: Read with a grain of salt. Seek written permission for what you **want to use.** How to use newsmagazines for the world scene. Quoting. Quote accurately.

Some handy references and how to use them. A reference librarian is a sharp cookie. Instant research.

12   *Plotting: First, Last, and Middle Chapters*   *84*

Sooner or later your novel must be plotted. The making of the blueprint. Three cheers for the easy way out. Letting stuff "flow" simply won't do. Don't waste energy. How to keep your plot interesting to your readers until they reach the end. How to get the reader's interest. Your rough notes for Chapter I. Doing the last chapter. *You* must know what the end will be. Aim for True North. Nothing is final yet. Your plotting notes tell you exactly what you have to do. Review each chapter. Time in plotting. Moving the novel forward. Exercise: How to block a published novel. Don't let your novel dawdle. Maintain momentum.

13   *Your Plotting Notebook for a Novel*   *91*

Time to plot. How to noodle your book. Introduce your characters one at a time. How to backtrack. A picture of your novel will emerge. Your outline supplies you with unexpected information. It is better to have noted than to have ignored. Hilda the paratrooper. Scatter your facts. Good plotting eliminates useless flashbacks. There are good flashbacks and bad flashbacks. Maintain the forward movement of the plot. Let the reader in on the action. Is something *really* happening? List your characters' reactions. How will Uncle Fuddles feel about being stuffed? Use your notebook. Make a page of reactions for every character. How to avoid those irritating situations. Inconsistencies. How to handle them. When you don't know what happens next. Why stew? Hilda and Herbert will survive. Have faith. The moment of truth—not enough happens! Don't quit. Start over. Plot a book that *is* a book.

14 *First, But Hardly Final Draft*   *100*

Books are not written in one sitting. Should you begin at the beginning? Bypassing the roadblocks. Your first draft is a raw and unfinished product. Don't dawdle. How to *make* the words come. When you polish, your prose will sing a sweet song. Your two pages a day will be no burden. You can't edit what you haven't written. Don't show your first draft to *anyone*. Like what you write but don't fall in love with each word and comma. Do your own typing. Don't throw away *anything* when you do your first draft. Write, write, write. Don't rest on your oars. Don't edit and polish now; that comes later. When you write your first draft, you have no time to spell. Correct later. Up and at 'em, genius!

15 *The Second Draft—Chapter by Chapter*   *107*

Tinkering with your first draft to get your second draft. Here's the way to work on it. Chapters can seldom be too short. A chapter is a unit. The scene as a chapter. The confrontation as a chapter. Cliff hangers. Scissors are handy gadgets. Read each chapter objectively.

Consider the physical setting. Can the reader visualize it? For now, put everything in your novel. The prize you seek is clarity. Read for dialogue. Turn long speeches into quick debates. Look at description. Break those solid blocks of description. This is the draft where you add to your book. The next draft is the draft you will hate.

16 *Ouch! The Art of Self-Editing* *113*

There is no way to make editing painless. Your manuscript won't heal itself; you have to edit the mess. How to make every page, sentence, and word sing. The general editing. Trim the fat. Use a yellow marker. Be cruel. Mark out anything that fails to move your plot forward. Get rid of useless adjectives and adverbs. Demand that each scene carry its own weight. If you've eliminated nothing, *don't* send your manuscript to a publisher. Good writers know when to throw the gems away. Now through the manuscript once again. Get rid of those flabby present participles. Make things happen. Cause and effect. Sort out your sentences. The periodic sentence. An overabundance of adverbs makes for sloppy writing. Watch *it*. Watch *its* and *it's* too. Possessives. Dirty words have lost their kick. Another obscenity is spelling. The hash we make of our writing. From hash comes clarity. Make haste slowly. Take a sabbatical. After a rest, read from start to finish again—objectively. Tinker some more. Stop. Stop cold. Time to kick the book out of the house. Ways to improve your kicking.

17   *Your Finished Novel—Where To Send It*   *127*

All those questions. How to prepare your manuscript. A good reason for carbons. Titles. How to send the manuscript to market. Sending a few chapters saves time. Can you copyright your script before you send it out? Sould you bind your manuscript? Should you write a letter? How to ship your book. Acknowledgement of your manuscript. What about paying to have your book published? Study the preferences of publishers. How to find out where to market your book. Pick a publishing house—and a second, and a third. One at a time. Do you need a lawyer? Do you need an agent? The agent who charges writers. Good-by to Hilda and Herbert. What to do now. Buy yourself another notebook. The name of the game.

Supplements

What A Novel Is   *141*

How To Get an Idea for Your Novel If
You Don't Already Have One   *148*

A Word about Viewpoint   *153*

Novel Markets   *157*

Index   *162*

Chapter 1

Watch That First Step—It's a Big One

You're going to write a novel? Welcome to the club! The club must be a whopper. If all who "plan someday to write a novel" *did* form a club, its national convention would include every two out of three people. And if they all *wrote* their books, holy mackerel!

I'm a free-lance writer who earns his keep from this delightful business. The thought that this horde might someday write those books should frighten me. Certainly many would be better than mine. I'd be out of business—fast. But I don't panic. I look forward to the day you finish your book. If your book is better than mine, congratulations. I am pleased—in a selfish way—that you plan to get started. With you in the picture, I'll have to work that much harder, and keep on my toes. You will make a better writer of me.

In the interim, may I offer you some tricks of the writing trade? I am a professional writer, but I don't presume to have all the answers. No writer worth his salt does. If we knew the score, we'd write nothing but best-selling masterpieces, and we don't do that. When writers help other writers it is the blind leading the blind. Maybe, with this help, you won't stumble as much as I did. But don't look for a magic wand. That went out with button shoes and the tooth fairy.

Actually, I can only suggest *one* method for you to write your novel: the way I write novels. Is my method a stunning success? Well, in two years I've sold four novels, I'm proud of them, and—as jazz men say— they keep me in bread. That may not answer your question, but it answers a lot of mine—especially the first of every month when the bills come in.

What works for me might not work for you. There are as many ways to write a novel as there are novelists. I presume to know only one: *my* way. I offer it here for this reason: I am fond of people who write as opposed to being fond of people who "talk" about writing. For instance, my lack of fondness for those who "talk" novels is such that when I am invited to give speeches about writing, I'm seldom invited back. Most would-be writers in these audiences are bores who babble nonsense. One asked me if he needed an agent in order to sell his novel to Hollywood. When I asked who published his book, he said he hadn't got around yet to writing it. The nut should have been home writing, but he got a bigger kick out of pretending to be a writer. I hope *you're* different. I hope you read this because you *must* write. If you read this to be amused, run out and buy a comic book. This is written expressly for those wonderful people who will pull a novel out of thin air the hard way—via sweat.

No one can promise you success or failure. You might follow my suggestions and write yourself a best-selling novel, end up terribly rich, have a yacht, summer cottages galore, eight sport cars, and credit with the Salvation Army. Or, your novel might wander from publisher to publisher and never find a home. What success or failure you have will be strictly your own doing. The point is, nobody can write your novel for you. Sooner or later you must stop thinking about it, and start writing it. The sooner the better. But when I say you *do* have a novel in you, I'm not flattering. We *all* have novels in us. Whether the novel stays in us or comes out, is up to us.

Aw, don't look glum. To write your book will be fun. To write a novel is almost as creative as having a baby—a point I make with no authority because we have, in our family, a division of labor. My wife has the babies and I have the books. Sooner or later you'll develop your own writing methods, but in lieu of anything better at the moment, perhaps my method will get you started.

Finding the 26-Hour Day

First we'll have to find those hours in which you can write each day. That's what the next chapter is about. Whether you're a housewife, husband, widow, widower, bachelor, or student, we'll find the hours you need. The next chapter will cheer you with this thought: to write a novel you won't have to write as much as you thought. If I'm lazy, you can be lazy, too. Every extra word we write—and don't use—is time wasted. Write efficiently—that's the motto of us lazy dogs. The next chapter won't teach you how to write when you have a headache but it does show that you can. In any event, when you finish that chapter you can say to yourself: "He *did* find extra hours. Now I *can* get started!"

Another early chapter lets you tinker with your novel's characters, shows you how to create them out of thin air, and—sad to say—tells you when to wad them up and throw them away. If you do as I do, you'll establish your characters right away, even before blocking out the plot that exists for them. Let the plot be loose at this point. If your novel possesses strong and delightful characters, they will take over and *help* you with your plotting. Things are not really *that* simple, but I approach my novels this way. Oh, I know the overall plot or I would not have begun, but you get the idea. Make haste slowly. Besides, it's fun to meet your characters, see the color of their eyes, and know what they eat for breakfast. When I have only a vague character in mind and must create his complete personality, I have a way—probably most unorthodox—to invent him. My way saves wear and tear on my imagination. And it's fast. I'll show you how to create a complete character in ten minutes and still have time for a cigarette. You'll also learn when and how to make characters from real live people so Aunt Tilly doesn't sue.

After you've established your characters, the next thing is to put words—and not your foot—in their mouths. Dialogue is not as treacherous as it might seem. You'll discover ways to make the conversations of your characters both reasonable and uncomplicated. They'll talk the way real people talk. Should you employ Uncle Ned's hilarious dialect? Should you make southern belles sound like country idiots? Relax. We'll tackle the dialogue problems you're most likely to encounter. We'll even investigate the art of eavesdropping which—if you're a cop, gossip, or writer—is a satisfying pastime. When does your novel have too much dialogue? When does it have too little? Stay tuned for Chapter Four.

Now if dialogue is not your Waterloo but description is, another chapter offers handy shortcuts which will help you describe this house, that town, or the sexy blonde who won't give you the time of day. The way I feel is, too much description is deadly. In fact, the less the better, but every sentence you do devote to description should be so vivid your reader can see, taste, hear, smell, and feel whatever you describe, allowing, of course, for propriety. Although you are probably familiar already with *Roget's Thesaurus,* you'll learn a few time-saving tricks not listed in the thesaurus itself. That alone is worth the price of admission.

Unless you're a Saudi Arabian or have been there a lot, forget about that blockbuster of a novel about oil rights. Anyway, the question of *where*—or the setting—for your novel is covered in another chapter. You'll find what pitfalls to avoid when describing a street or a city. Since I stumbled into every one handy—and some I went out of my way to reach—you'll at least be further along in the writing game than I was. Another chapter illustrates how easy research can be. More power to those lucky souls who spend years to research a book, but if you're working full-time, you haven't the years to fritter away. You'll find out how to compress months of research into a few evenings at the public library.

Chapters Seven, Eight, and Nine deal with how to put into your novel: pizzazz, sex, and humor. Pizzazz? That's Madison Avenue's word for finding a new way to make ordinary things happen and thus hold the reader's interest. As for sex in novels, I have strong views on how much or little actual sex is needed. Fundamentally, I'm a cross between a Puritan and the Marquis de Sade, with a little of Louisa May Alcott for a chaser. No matter. Your own views will be as definite —and as different—as mine. This is about how to write a novel, not how to reform or be a free spirit. Although I will not tell you how to write a dirty book because I think they're more dull than dirty, I will pass along a few thoughts on how to make bedroom scenes more credible. Humor, being trickier than sex, offers many blind alleys, none of which I have been able to ignore, but I'll try to list a few in the hope you are wiser than I am. One chapter deals with, if you have such, your Great Message. You'll learn how to change it from a rambling night letter to a telling ten-word telegram. The same chapter traffics with the problem all writers face: whether to impose their personalities on the novel or to remain detached. The first—done poorly—slows the plot and the second—done poorly—is awfully Noel Cowardish in a sophomoric way. The truth is, no writer can keep from exposing himself when he writes a novel. Sooner or later, who and what he is comes through.

Building Your Story—A Step At A Time

Plotting is important. That's what novels are about. I will not deny that the thought of plotting a novel—chapter after chapter—gives one pause. But don't let the prospect throw you. To walk ten miles is equally exhausting. For the stroll, you take one step at a time. You don't walk the full ten miles at once. When you plot, you keep the overall design of your novel in mind, but you plot one chapter at a time. So relax. We'll plot together. You'll be surprised how simple—and efficient— plotting is. If you can plan a dinner, you can plot a novel. If you can plan a hunting junket, you can plot a novel. If you're incapable of either, don't despair. If you can plan your days so you don't run out of socks, you can plot a novel.

After your novel is plotted, the fun begins. You begin to write it. The moment you do you'll discover there's no such animal as inspiration. And don't expect help from a good fairy, either. You'll learn there's no such animal as "writer's block"—that dreadful day when words are not supposed to flow. "Writer's block" in my opinion is another word for laziness. Other and better writers will take issue with me on this, so listen to both sides, and make up your own mind. But use "writer's block" as an excuse when talking to them. Don't tell me about it, I'll give you another stony look. When the first draft is done, we'll begin your second—which, once again, is not as awful as it sounds. You'll simply edit the first draft, add here, subtract there, feel ill at times, and be filled with glee other times. You may cut your first draft into a jigsaw puzzle to rearrange it completely. You might end the way you started, you might not, but you'll never know until you try. Once your jigsaw puzzle is tacked together again you'll edit the third draft for grammar and efficiency, cutting every word, sentence, and paragraph that makes your novel bog. This, also, is not as terrible or as complicated as it sounds. It's easier to do than say. When you've finished the third draft you'll find that your fifth grade English teacher would be proud of you. You know more about grammar now than you think you do. By then, you'll be the expert my obnoxious son is.

We both cross our fingers at that point and hope a publisher feels the way your English teacher does, because by then your script is ready to be typed on good bond paper and shipped away—to sink or swim in the grown up world of books.

We'll also cover—thoroughly—the many things that face you when your book is ready for final typing. We'll tackle some important questions:

How do you prepare your manuscript for market?
How do you ship it?
Where do you ship it, to agent or to publisher?
Can you copyright it?

We'll also explain what happens when cheerful souls say:

"For a price, pal, I'll whip your script into shape."

Or:

"For a price, pal, we'll publish your book."

The only thing this piece of writing you're holding right now won't do is tuck you into bed and write your novel for you. Nobody can do that. I can give you my views on the questions that trouble you, and other writers might answer your questions differently, but whether you agree with me or disagree, is unimportant. Write the novel that's in you. If, at times, you hit lonely days, suffer a little. They say suffering is good for the soul. I have days like that, too. Now and then I stare at this typewriter, brood, and wonder if I should have stayed in the military. I joined in 1942. I might be a corporal by now and I hear the pay is good.

I also have the feeling I would have been a great tap dancer—had I ever learned to dance. Just remember one thing: whatever happens at that typewriter of yours, you're not alone.

Chapter 2

How To Write a Novel in One Hundred Days

When—oh, *when!*—will you find time to write?

If you're not a housewife whose days are filled with dirty dishes, you're her husband who works eight hours in salt mines to come home to a faucet to fix. If you're neither, then you're a teenager, college grind, bachelor, widow, widower, or that beautiful typist trying to catch a man. To all, I offer sympathy. None of you has time to write. Feel better?

(Now offer *me* sympathy. As I write this I have a combination summer cold and headache, got in late last night, longed to sleep forever, but it is six hours later, and here I sit at this monster typewriter. . .Grow up. The fact is, no one *ever* had time to write a novel. So where do novels come from? From writers who *make* time to write— that's where. Look around you. Everybody and his brother write novels they haven't time to write. Housewives make time to write. Husbands make time to write. Students make time to write. Grandmothers make time to write. The cop on the corner is making time to write and so is the robber he nailed last week. Don't moan about no time to write. If you want to write—*must* write—you can make time, too.

Granted, to write a book is awesome. Takes lots of paper, too. If to write a ten-page short story is a major task, to write a book that runs two hundred to a thousand pages seems well nigh impossible, doesn't it? Between *Chapter One* and *The End* you will have put reams of paper through your typewriter and several seasons might have flitted by. Have you the audacity to begin? To start a book takes a certain amount of audacity. To complete the book takes even more. Where will the time come from? If you rent an ivory tower, hide there and write your heart out, your family will starve. Nobody will send *Care* packages. Get that through your noodle here and now.

(Relax a minute, will you? My head is splitting. Know what I'd like? A quiet lake is five minutes away. I'd like to forget writing and everything. I'd like to go to that lake, drench myself in silence, and snooze. But I haven't the time. You see, you are not alone. . .)

Before we find those hours you need to write, let me make a suggestion. Forget about writing blockbuster novels that dress down to ten pounds and ten hundred pages. Most of them are better doorstops than novels. Why pour your soul into a book that may cause a slipped disc? Such books require thousands of manuscript pages. Common sense should tell you that you can write a thousand-page manuscript and still get rejection slips. A thousand is a thousand—which is not too brilliant a conclusion unless you look at a thousand pages this way: you can write a shorter novel in less time. While Charlie Paperwaster writes one thousand-page tome, you could write five two-hundred page novels. Since you'll have written five to his one, check the track odds. You're a five-to-one favorite. If four of your novels bomb, so what? You sell your fifth; he's still slipping a disc from his first. So be sensible. Set your sights on a book with two to three hundred manuscript pages. Better to peddle *five* lightweight novels at five dollars apiece than one heavyweight tome for ten. Fair enough? So now you can breathe easier. You planned to write a thousand pages. You have only to write two hundred.

"But *where* can I find time to write them?" you say.

I thought you'd never ask.

My friend, I hope this will come as no surprise: there are twenty-four hours in each day. I'll grant that you have work to do. Housewives work at home and sometimes elsewhere, too. Husbands work. Students work. Everybody works. Today even I am working, and I don't feel up to it. We can't avoid work. Poets these days work. They must: garrets rent for more and the price of cheese is up. But the day still has twenty-four hours. How do you waste yours? Let's say you spend eight of those hours—five or six days a week—in the salt mines, another hour or so getting to and from home, and after you allow yourself time to eat and sleep, the day is used up. In other words, you don't have ten hours a day to work on your novel. I'll buy that if you buy this: since you have so little free time, you must use that free time efficiently.

In other words, be mean to yourself. Order yourself—with no time off for good behavior—to write at least two pages a day for the next one hundred days. At the end of those one hundred days you will have written at least two hundred pages, improved your typing speed, and alienated several of your friends, but you will have the satisfaction of knowing the first draft of your novel is an accomplished fact. The look in you eye suggests this is easier said than done. The look implies that I have gone round the bend.

Commit Yourself

Look at it this way. To write a book takes the same discipline as to go on a diet. Both are easy to put off. But let's pretend you really *want* to write your novel. Let's pretend the only roadblock you face is time. Do this. Broadcast loud and clear to family, friends, and whoever will listen that come hell or high water for the next one hundred days you are going to write at least two pages a day. Brag how, at the end of those one hundred days, you'll have completed the first draft of your novel. Accept the ooh's and ah's with modesty, smile at each scoffer, but make a Hollywood production of your intentions. After that, the going is easy. All you have to do is write or you'll never hear the end of it. Nothing like the sour look of your neighbor to make you trim your hedge or write your book.

When in each day you choose to write your two pages only you can determine. I am an early morning writer myself. You might do better to burn the midnight oil. If you're working eight hours a day, get up two hours earlier and write before you go to work. Or, write when the kids are bedded for the night. If you can write after dark and into the wee hours I will not pretend to understand. I will only admire your ability. I, myself, can't write after dinner. By the time the table is cleared, I'm yawning to beat the band. But if you're a night writer, so be it. Just make sure you write your two pages before you hit the sack. If you're not certain when you write better—early morning or late at night—do this. Try one way for two weeks. Then, try the other way. Then no one will have to tell you when the stuff flows faster. You'll know.

(Interesting discovery: I *can* type while sneezing and suffering from the ache-all-over feeling of a cold. . .)

Whenever you write, *write*. Dawdling is deadly. Don't stare at your typewriter and procrastinate, brood about movie royalties, or wonder if you strike it rich whether to summer in Spain or Mexico. Write! Dawdle on your own time, daydream during dinner, but when you sit down to write, forget about the dirty *e* on the typewriter. Start right off and *write*. Write what? Write anything that pertains to your novel. Don't worry about what. Later on we'll tackle the problem of plotting. You'll have more things to write than you can shake a stick at. Don't write any of that lazy, brown dog jazz. Doesn't sell. Perhaps you might pick up writing where you left off the day before. Or, should that not strike your fancy, you might write a few pages of description that does. If you're more in the mood to write this scene than that scene, by all means, write the scene you choose. For the moment forget about chronological order. True, your novel must eventually travel in an orderly manner from beginning to middle to end, but not at this point. Neatness comes with the final typing, not the first draft. If you wish to write the last chapter first, more power to you. When you ship the script to market put the chapters in the right order—and that's all there is to it. If you can write your two pages fast, great. Take time off and dream a little. Or, write a few more pages. If the writing comes slow, that's tough. Stay at the typewriter until two pages are written. Keep on schedule. Whatever you do, don't daydream at the typewriter. Untyped daydreams don't sell.

"It's impossible," you mutter," to sit right down and start writing. Writing isn't that easy for me. I have to think about what I'm going to say."

Think Before You Sit Down At the Typewriter

True, true, true. But not while you're typing those two pages. Plan ahead. For instance, consider this chapter, the one you're now reading. I didn't stagger from my bed to the typewriter and start typing. First, I staggered around the house for an hour, drank black coffee, wished I were dead, read the morning paper, and—also—jotted notes for this chapter. By the time I arrived at the typewriter I had a fistful of notes, a terrible headache, and a hacking cough. Then I started to put one word after another. Soon a paragraph was completed, then a page, then a handful of pages—and here we are. Had I waited at the typewriter for inspiration, I'd still be on page one or cleaning the typewriter keys. Better to employ your free moments *away* from the typewriter to toy with what you plan to write. Be efficient the next one hundred days. Make *every* moment count.

If you're a housewife doing dishes, do you concentrate on that task? No. You've mastered dishwashing. You work without thinking. So use that time to think about what you're going to write next. Same is true when you're waxing the floor. Wear out your brain as well as your back. Kill two birds with one stone. Going to the salt mines each day? Don't read the morning paper on the bus or train. Jot down notes of things to write next. Ignore your fellow workers for a hundred days and eat lunch by yourself. Chew and think. Skip your favorite television show. The station will rerun it—time and again. Think. Think about what you're going to write next.

Do this and I promise you that when you sit down at your typewriter you'll have so much to write you won't worry about the dirty *e*. You might surprise yourself and get up a real head of steam, writing five or six pages instead of two. Just make sure you write those two. Keep on schedule. That's all I ask.

What about Saturday and Sunday when you have the full day free? On such days to turn out two required pages is easy as pie. But hold on. Put down the fishing equipment. Use these two days, in addition, to review the pages you wrote that week. Or, use that free time for research; we'll get to that soon.

Where you write is, of course, your business. I would suggest, however, you don't choose the living room when the television is going full blast. Don't choose the kitchen table, either. You'll be asked to carry out the garbage. Hide in the bathroom if you must, lock yourself in a bedroom, or go somewhere in the car—alone—and park. Use the public library. You probably won't be able to type there but you can scribble in longhand, can't you? If you do, better scribble four pages a day instead of two. When your scribbling is typed you will end up with the two pages required. The important thing about where to write is to pick a place where no one can bother you. One interruption always leads to another, soon you'll be behind schedule, and there will be your neighbor, leaning over the back fence, braying that you are a loudmouth.

Your worst enemies are those who love you. I know because I am surrounded by such enemies. Prepare to be surrounded by them too. Your spouse will say, "Honey, you've been working awfully hard. You should rest. Take it easy for awhile." Oh, how pleasant to agree to *that* suggestion—especially today the my head feels. Or, your children will say, "Come play with us." Happily, under any circumstances I find that invitation distasteful, but when I'm stuck with a plot, their offer tempts me. A neighbor will call, "Come over for a beer!" Well-meaning souls, tempters all! "The grass needs cutting," your wife will say. "Busy!" you shout, which settles her hash. Other temptations are not easy to ignore. "Hey, your favorite television program is starting!" But ignore them all we must if we are to be efficient. All work and no play makes novels. Beer will keep, television will come around again, and who wants to cut grass! Simply put, don't be fooled by the good intentions of those who love you. Your loved ones are your enemy. Anything that hinders your writing schedule needs to be growled at.

No Holidays for Novelists

I am aware as you soon will be that another enemy of any writing schedule is the national holiday, be it Labor Day, Thanksgiving, or Christmas. Realize from the start that not everyone in your home will share your enthusiasm for the typewriter. After the first few weeks prepare for their enthusiasm to wane—fast—especially if a national holiday is just around the corner. In their well-ordered world, national holidays are to be celebrated. Scrooge, the patron saint of writers, said bah humbug to holidays, but I haven't seen him around much lately. I'm afraid we're on our own and surrounded by well-meaning people who say: "At least take the Fourth of July off!" Or take Christmas off, Easter, Ground Hog Day, or the second anniversary of Aunt Tilly's gallstone operation. Holidays to non-writers mean just that: *holidays.*

Somewhere in the course of your one hundred days, a national holiday will pop up. As you sit at your typewriter, faced with the day free and clear, your spouse will call, "Come downstairs, dear. It's Christmas." Or: "Dinner's waiting. It's Thanksgiving, stupid!" Which call you answer—the typewriter or the turkey—depends on you. You'll have to decide for yourself. This is only reasonable. You were the one who picked your one hundred days. Waste them if you like.

But know this: if you stretch those one hundred days into one day more, you'll get no sympathy from me. I'll be with your neighbor, leaning over your fence, and braying:

"Who were you kidding? You'll never write that novel. You couldn't even finish the first draft!"

What I mean is, if I can write this chapter the way *I* feel, you can write a novel—dozens of them, in fact.

Chapter 3

Creating An Unforgettable Character

Now, let's get started.

Common sense tells you that you can't begin *anywhere* until you know what your novel is about. This "what your novel is about" is the seed from which your novel grows.

(If you don't already know what you want to write a novel about, it might be a good idea to review the Supplement on page 148 before going any further.)

If you *do* have at least an idea, how do you know whether it's worth a novel or whether it would hold up as even a short story—or a joke at your next coffee break? The deciding is not always easy. Nor is the explaining. But briefly, and chiefly:

A novel idea has a greater scope than a short story idea. That is, you have more room to manuever in a novel. So you have room for a cast of screaming thousands if that's the sort of thing you like in your novels. Or, you can take a character from birth, or back into his ancestry, to death and beyond (you should know him well enough to know where he's going). If, then, your idea is large and sweeping, asquirm with plots sub and counter, if its time span is great—from when Aunt Tillie was a bashful young stowaway on that oil tanker, through her courtship by the handsome young pirate, who turns out to be the son of the shipping magnate who owns the oil tanker, to when, as a society matron, she gives the tea party that enchants all Boston, you probably have a novel. If, on the other hand, your idea concerns what happens to tiny Bobby Glotz when he takes his piggy bank to the corner drugstore to buy a gallon jug of peony perfume for his mother's birthday and then heroically breaks the jug over the head of a fleeing bank robber, who, because of Bobby's selfless sacrifice is subsequently traced to his lair by the stench of peonies, that's probably a short story. Or a short-short story. Or a lie told by Bobby Glotz's demented mother. The difference between the novel idea and the short story idea is one of scope.

Time is of the essence, but time is not the only thing. *Ulysses* takes place within a single 24-hour day, but it has the scope of a novel because it treats the 24-hour day across the entire landscape of the mind. The difference is, maybe, leisure to explore the ideas involved at length. A short story has time only to bring a single idea dramatically to a climax. The crisis usually is a single, personal one for the principal character. A novel can explore, write more variations on a theme, digress to emphasize its meaning. A short story has time only to sing the tune, once through.

Now that you know what your novel will be about—you know also some of the characters your novel requires. At this point, dealer's choice. You can begin your novel one way or another. You can begin by plotting—that is, noting what must happen chapter after chapter. Or, you can begin with characterization—that is, creating three-dimensional characters from a handful of words. While trying to decide which way you will start to work, don't go into a tizzy. Either way is okay.

My preference is characterization, so if you'd rather plot your novel before doing that, jump ahead to the chapters on plotting. Return to this chapter some other time. If you want to noodle with characters first, read on.

No matter how many characters your novel will have, chances are after your book is published some bumpkin will look at you and say:

"But which character was really *you*?"

Although such questions are compliments, you'll feel like belting him. You wrote the novel. You put words into the mouths of *all* your characters. You made them cry, travel, drink coffee, dream, stub toes, feel pain, find joy, get married, and—at times—die. While you might borrow your character from real life, the depository of *all* characters, nonetheless your fictional Aunt Tilly is not the real-life Aunt Tilly who ran off with the tattoo artist. God—not you—created the real Aunt Tilly, and God created the tattoo artist, too. That's the way real life is.

True, in your novel you play God a little. You make fictional Aunt Tilly what she is—or isn't. You make every character in your novel that way, too. So which character in your book is you? *All* of them. They speak your words, operate on streets you thought up, and when the cry, they use your tears.

Creating fictional characters and playing God to them is an exercise filled with joy and grief. Your "paper" people will become as real to you as flesh-and-blood people. What your characters feel, you will feel —only more intensely. When they feel pain, you'll feel pain and then some. When they feel happiness, you—being the creator of their happiness—will know more happiness than they dreamed possible. They will have the babies but you will have their labor pains. They will die but you will experience death. They will kiss but you will experience their passion. Why is this? Because if you don't feel twice whatever they feel, you will not be able to create that feeling in them at all. So much is lost in the translation. Our emotions are most inefficient. Emotions are too fragile to communicate fully. Between you and your reader your fictional Aunt Tilly stands. If your reader is to know joy, you must heap joy into Aunt Tilly's heart. And for you to heap joy there, you must experience the wonder of joy as well as its mechanical parts. Aunt Tilly will feel only a fraction of what you want her to feel, and—sad but true —your reader will feel only a fraction of what Aunt Tilly feels. So choke up when she does. If you don't, she won't, and your reader never will.

Since your novel will contain more characters than one Aunt Tilly, prepare to suffer the torments of the damned. Aunt Tilly suffers only for herself. You must suffer for her and all her friends. Fair warning: the moment you don't feel emotion toward a character you've created, start over or become a hack. You won't have created a character. You will have only typed—and wasted—words.

They say writing is a lonely craft, but I dispute that premise. True, we spend hours at these typewriters, we daydream, and we have no time for back-fence chats. But lonely? No, no, no. Once a minister—meaning well, I suppose—said I should "get out more and meet people." I had been holed up for days, mumbling through meals, not answering letters, dodging telephone calls, and refusing to answer the door. My mind, then, was somewhere else: sorting out sentences, characters, and descriptions. "Meet more people," the minister said. Meet people? At that precise moment I was involved intimately in the lives of eight characters in a novel. Worse, I was solely responsible for every last one of them. I didn't need another soul and I certainly wasn't lonely. Create characters correctly and you won't be lonely either. Others might think so, but you'll know better. And consider this pleasant thought: in many ways fictional characters are better than their real-life counterparts; how many real-life people can you wad up and throw away?

Consider our fictional Aunt Tilly, who—as I write this—does not exist. What will make her come to life can make your characters come to life. At this moment we know nothing about her. Mark this moment well. This will be the only moment that you, I, and the reader are on equal footing. Just as we have questions about who Aunt Tilly is and what makes her tick, so has the reader. The difference is, the reader will wait for us to supply the answers. Very well, let's suppose our novel needs an Aunt Tilly but let's suppose also that we feel adventurous. We won't borrow our Aunt Tilly from real life. We want to fabricate her out of thin air—and in ten minutes. Big order? Nope. Watch us work.

One Way to Start

First, to fix Aunt Tilly somewhere in time (she must have an age!) we'll play a game. Tear up pieces of paper. On each, write a number: twenty through sixty. Put the numbers in a hat, shake well, pull one out, and there we are: her age! That tells us something but not much. Let's find out more. Toss a coin—heads mean yes, tails mean no—to see if she is, or isn't, married. Is she cheerful or hateful? Toss the coin and see. Is she beautiful or a hag? Flip and see. A sexpot or cold fish? Democrat or Republican? A good housekeeper or slatternly? Married or not, does she chase men or is she a one-man woman? Is she intellectual or fluff? Does she dress in style or Sears rejects? Does she eat exotic or plain fare? Toss the coin, list your answers, and witness Aunt Tilly's emergence as a three-dimensional person unlike any other. We asked questions readers might ask. And we saved time by flipping a coin.

For instance, on the strength of the game, our Aunt Tilly could be twenty-three years old, married, and a cheerful Republican who chases men, dresses fancy, but eats plain. On the other hand Aunt Tilly could have emerged as a thirty-four year old hag who is married, keeps a filthy house but eats only chocolate covered ants, and hates all men including her lucky husband. Even when you borrow bits and pieces of your character from real life make up a list as we did here. Just make up questions which will be more central to your plot needs. You will thus create a three-dimensional character unlike any mother used to make.

Here's another trick. To know your characters as well as you know yourself, write a letter to someone (you?) and describe the Aunt Tilly we just fabricated. When you write letters you don't brood about literary flair do you? You simply write it. That's all you do here. But describe your fictional Aunt Tilly so well that whoever reads the letter could say, "Yeah, I can almost see . . ." Tell the color of her eyes and how tall she is. Did she mingle at the party where you met, or did she slink to a corner to sulk? Describe imaginary arguments with her in which she takes firm stands on youth, the war, fluoridation, sex, books, husbands, and Amelia Earhart. Pick the subjects you like or need for your novel. Real people have grubby attitudes on everything, don't they? Let Aunt Tilly have them, too. This is Be Kind To Aunt Tilly Week.

To make Aunt Tilly even more human, dip into history. You know when she was born because you know her age. Well, when she first squinted at the world about her, what did she see: horsecars or jet planes? If she was born before Pearl Harbor she might feel one way about Medicare. If she was born before World War One she might have strong views on rock-and-roll music. If she was born during the Korean War she won't feel about Guy Lombardo as I do. List which years she was in grade school. List the time in history she went through adolescence. What was happening then? A war? A depression? Or what? These items shaped our characters. They'll shape Aunt Tilly's, too.

Do this with *all* your characters.

Know more about your characters than you can use in your novel.

You can't know too much about them. Know them intimately, then when you turn them loose in the plot, you'll be in for happy surprises. The day will come when you sit at your typewriter as only a spectator. Your hands will type words, but Aunt Tilly will have a mind of her own. She will say and do things that surprise and please you. When you want her to say a thing one way, she'll say it another—and better—way. When you want her to react in Manner A, she will react in Manner B. You will have the uneasy feeling your fictional Aunt Tilly has come alive. You will almost be able to hear her scold:

"You created me, but I'm *me,* now. Keep your cotton-picking thoughts to yourself."

Believe me, when that moment comes—and if you write with your heart that moment *will* come—you will feel like celebrating. Suddenly your novel will be fired with a life of its own—and away it goes! Don't expect that moment to arrive too soon, and don't try to force it. Sometimes I have played at this typewriter for months, feeling sad and useless, working with this or that character. But the character kept saying what *I* wanted him to say. He was still doing what *I* wanted him to do. He was not a flesh-and-blood character doing what he must. I have learned to keep going anyway, keep typing and wait for the moment my character comes to life. Yours will, too. Then your fingers will race over the typewriter keys. You will be the spectator at an event your characters make happen. They will no longer be an accumulation of mannerisms from here and there; they will be *themselves.*

Caution: keep your head on your shoulders when, all about you, your characters are losing theirs. Don't allow a minor character, however charming, to take over the plot. And, just as bad, don't let your main character take the plot a direction you don't wish the plot to travel. Quarrel with Aunt Tilly about this. If she persists, yank the page from the typewriter, wad it up, throw it away, and start over. Aunt Tilly will get the message.

What About Using Real People?

Can you use real people as characters in your novel? By this, of course, you mean can you take Aunt Tilly—the real life Aunt Tilly—off the front porch and drop her—kerplunk!— onto a page? When writing a biography or autobiography, the more real people the better. In fact, they're essential if you live in the world the rest of us do. But what of putting your real Aunt Tilly into fiction? Will she object? People never seem to like their own photographs; they feel the same about "word portraits" too. "That couldn't be me," they whine when they stare at snapshots. When they read fiction, they are the same. "Is that me he's writing nasty things about?" they whine. Or, if they don't whine, they kick you where you live, or sue. When crossed, the real-life Aunt Tilly can be a tiger.

So should you use her? Chance it. That's my advice. Nothing you or anyone will write can capture the *real* Aunt Tilly. We see her from the outside. She's in there, looking out. We know some of the things that make her tick, but not all. Not even her hair dresser knows. If you want to use her, do it this way. Borrow her speech pattern, seductive waddle, or whatever strikes your fancy. Borrow a cupful of her likes and dislikes while you're at it. Now, try this: Add to this conglomeration a cupful of the likes and dislikes of Uncle Fuddles. Add a few mannerisms of your own because, subconsciously you would have anyway. Mix these items well, and there's a fictional Aunt Tilly the real one will never recognize. Your fictional character, in fact, will be such a composite of so many people the real Aunt Tilly will mutter:

"Wish you'd put *me* in a book someday. . ."

Your fictional Aunt Tilly must have a name, but tread with care. If, in real life, her name *is* Aunt Tilly, change her fictional name to Aunt Emma. Why court henbane in your soup or a law suit? If her name in real life is Brown, don't name your fictional Aunt Tilly Black, Green, or any other color. When in doubt, use Smith—unless her last name *is* Smith *or* Jones. In that case, don't call her either. Call her Brown. Do you see? If you use the real name or an "opposite" that strikes you as brilliant, you ask for trouble. Why change real-life Ted Brown to Ned Brown? Marie Jones in real life is dangerously similar to Mary Jones, isn't it? If you can dream up plots, you can dream up names for your characters.

If you can't, use the telephone book which has more last names than we could think of in a million years.

When creating Aunt Tilly employ specifics to make her more human. Sweeping generalizations are dandy in essays, but today's readers require *details*. Sabatini, writing about Scaramouche, said, "He was born with a gift of laughter and a sense that the world was mad." If you're another Sabatini, well and good. But for the time being, let's pretend you're not. Let's pretend you plan to write a novel about people and things you know—and so few of us know kings these days. Scaramouche might have had a "sense that the world was mad" but more than likely your characters, although as universal, will be less encompassing. To them the world isn't mad, the cop on the corner is. Your reader wants to know what *specifically* makes Aunt Tilly laugh. Name three things. Why *specifically* does she consider the world mad? Name three things, and don't just say, "Because of the way things are." *What* things ? And what way are they? Does she seethe because of student riots? Or because a waitress ignores her? Which paragraph tells us more about Aunt Tilly:

> 1. Aunt Tilly hates grubby boys with runny noses, walking barefoot in the grass, and young mothers who smoke, but, on the other hand, she worships the ground Rudy Vallee walks on.
> 2. Aunt Tilly does not like certain children, certain uninhibited acts, and certain modern mothers, but she favors many things past.

Both paragraphs cover the same ground, but the first tells us specifically about Aunt Tilly and the second tells us lamely about some people. Aunt Tilly is not a bunch of people. Aunt Tilly is herself. When she hates, let her hate something specific. The same is true when she loves. Does she love pinboys or bone china? Real people have specific likes and dislikes, don't they? Why deprive Aunt Tilly? You and I don't wander through the day with our minds filled only with generalities, do we? One minute we're irritated because the waitress forgot our coffee. Fifteen minutes later we are debating the overwhelming question of how much to tip. None of these items is earth-shaking and they're not Grand Generalizations or Pithy Platitudes. Generalizations and platitudes we save for parties. They are the meat upon which such gatherings feed. In real life we march straight from breakfast to bedtime involved with specifics and our reactions to them. Aunt Tilly is the same.

Don't overload your characters with so many Deep Meanings they have little time to worry about a broken shoe string. True, the total of our lives has Deep Meanings, but any total is the sum of its parts. Now and then we stop wondering about eternity to wonder if we put out the cat.

Don't Forget This Handy Tool

When describing Aunt Tilly, break out your thesaurus. Why exhaust yourself trying to think up ways to describe her? Suppose she is angry all the time. Look up *Anger* in your thesaurus. You will find that Aunt Tilly can walk around filled with resentment, displeasure, irritation, annoyance, aggravation, and exasperation. This is better than using *angry* every time she enters, isn't it? From morning to night she can be in (choice of one) a *high dudgeon*, a *huff*, a *pique*, or a *tizzy*. Don't forget *tiff* and *miff*. A few pages later she can *have a conniption* or *fly into a rage*. Her soul can be filled alternatively with *fury, vehemence*, or a mixed bag of *towering rage, raging passion*, or *tearing passion*. You can tell *specifically* what anger makes her do: *redden, flush, growl, snarl, snap, grind her teeth, champ at the bit, give dirty looks*, or *look daggers*. Instead of saying she is *angry*, now and then let her *seethe, burn, simmer, sizzle, smolder, fume, stew, boil, fret, foam at the mouth*, and—a few pages later, she can *breathe fire, kick up a row*, or *stamp her foot*. Consider the many things Aunt Tilly can get up besides her *anger*: she can get her *dander, Irish, back*, and *hair* up. She can *bridle, bristle up, flare up, blaze up, flame up*, and when not doing those charming things, she can *fly off the handle, hit the ceiling, blow her stack*, or *explode*. See what I mean? Why stick with *anger*? Try to create such a list on your own and you'll waste valuable time. The thesaurus is a handy tool. Learn how to use it. I wrote this paragraph—and compiled this list for Aunt Tilly's anger—in fifteen minutes. It took so long because I stopped for a cigarette. Without the thesaurus this list might have taken me days—and I'd have missed many of the words.

What works for anger works for joy—and any other emotion or character trait Aunt Tilly possesses. Use your thesaurus. The English language has many apt words. Use them. Why skimp?

Every time a new character is introduced, some authors—happily, not many—stop the action of their novel. What follows is page after page of description, beautifully written, but easily skipped. Don't let the reader skip a word you write. Insist he read every word on every page lest he miss something. Readers read novels for the story—the plot—and anything that slows the story, they ignore. Lengthy descriptions of characters fall into this category. The author says, "We'll get on with the story in a few minutes. Meanwhile let me tell you how Aunt Tilly *really* is. . ." The reader skips these paragraphs as easily as you and I skip television commercials. When the announcer says, "We'll be back after these messages. . ." off we go. We have become a nation of people who can go to the bathroom in sixty seconds. Point is, never give your reader the opportunity to set your book aside—or to skip pages. Soon he'll skip more. If he sets your book aside, he might not return to it.

Describe Aunt Tilly with no more than a sentence here, a brief paragraph there, but never in one fell swoop. You might even prepare your reader in advance for her entrance. Use the tried-and-true theatrical device. Before she appears let your characters talk about her. And fill in some of her description by noting any reaction to her the other characters have. In any event, *do* describe her. Let the reader know who she is, what she had for breakfast, and the color of her eyes. Then, get on with your plot. Come back later and color her in.

Be careful with Aunt Tilly. Never let her get out of character. Make sure, when she opens her mouth, you don't put your foot in it. If Aunt Tilly drinks, don't have her rave about Carrie Nation. If Aunt Tilly is a fifteen-year-old, don't have her recite Einstein's theory. If Aunt Tilly is an ancient, don't have her mooning over Tab Hunter. In other words, what Aunt Tilly says or does must be the sort of thing she—and not some one else—would say or do. This may sound obvious, but it's a trap. Such traps can scuttle Aunt Tilly and all your characters.

I know, I know! If you *must* write things your characters would never say, go ahead and write them. Get these ill-timed harangues out of your system. Then, once they're out of your system, edit them out of your novel.

As suggested at the start of this chapter, all the characters in your novel are you. You breathe life into them and they respond by being, on paper, *real* people. What we have done here with Aunt Tilly, I would suggest you do with every character your novel contains. Perhaps the questions we asked of Aunt Tilly—and answered by flipping a coin— are not the questions you would ask of your characters. That makes sense because they are not the questions I would ask of mine, either. Each character suggests its own list of questions, doesn't it?

Don't sit around and wait for inspiration to strike. Characters aren't created by wishing on stars or baying at the moon. No character ever saw the light of day as the result of a magic wand. So get started—now. Fill in your characters. Make them real. Use whatever timesavers you wish—the flip of a coin, thesaurus, or the telephone book. These things and not inspiration will make your characters come to life on paper. Inspiration is something you make happen. So are your characters. I wish you and your characters well. As for Aunt Tilly, she's served her purpose. Let's wad her up and throw her away.

Chapter 4

It Takes Two to Dialogue

"You're kidding!"

"Nope. Guess again."

"But you must be kidding. Writers don't use dialogue for *that*!"

"*I* do."

"Holy mackerel!"

And there you are: conversation. Between whom? Between a reader and myself. I explained to him the reason I use a lot of dialogue in my books. Perhaps I shouldn't have told him though. I hate to be tricked, and readers feel the same; but for better or for worse one of the tricks in the writing trade is dialogue. For example, I use dialogue to keep the reader tuned in. To begin a chapter with dialogue immediately carries the reader, ready or not, forward in the plot. When Chapter M closed, Hilda and Herbert were holding hands and giggling. Chapter N opens, Hilda and Herbert are nowhere in sight, but Uncle Fuddles is haggling with George Washington. I figure that if movies and television can cut abruptly from scene to scene so can the novelist. Or, if we're writing a long-winded blockbuster, we don't use the ploy. We send the lovers home, make the moon go down, order the sun to rise, give the milkman a few paragraphs of philosophy to spout, describe the dawn (usually rosy-fingered), plop the morning paper on the porch, and on and on. But if you prefer a swifter novel that eliminates trivia, the surefire way to efficiency is dialogue.

Dialogue, you see, is this chapter's subject.

"It is?"

"Of course it is. Where've you been?"

"Well, if you must know, I sort of scanned the last paragraph and. . ."

Don't apologize. Writers are like readers. Blocks of type called paragraphs make heavy reading, don't they? Dialogue is more effective because dialogue is less like a lecture. When confronted with a straight paragraph of exposition, the reader can only agree or disagree. Dialogue, on the other hand, usually presents two or more points of view and the reader has someone on his side, arguing back.

Unless you read books for the sexy sections, you'll favor the novel with the most dialogue. To flip through a novel that contains page after page of solid paragraphs makes you wonder which the book is: a novel or a diatribe. So do as I do. Make your novel *easier* to read. Use dialogue—pages and pages of it. Dialogue makes the reader feel he's where the action is.

Dialogue is the novelist's friend another way, too. You plan to fill two hundred pages or so with writing, don't you? Which uses more space and takes *less* writing: dialogue or a paragraph of exposition? Dialogue, of course. Dialogue fills pages quickly, so be lavish with conversation. Use conversation every time you turn around—and don't worry. You can never have too much dialogue in a novel.

"I can't?"

"That's what I said, my friend."

"Fine, but what about right here, on *this* page? Why dialogue? Seems like you're wasting space."

"No. Apt dialogue doesn't waste space. What we're doing here, you and I, illustrates how a spot of dialogue now and then breaks the monotony of too many paragraphs."

"Ah."

Example: now and then, being human, we all get carried away with description. Our deathless prose, studded with adjectives, goes on and on. Our prose stops the forward movement of the plot, and that is a sin. So while we wax poetic, what can we do to save the day and hold the reader? Slip in a dash of dialogue every few paragraphs, that's what. Let's say we're describing Hilda. We write three paragraphs of prose that would make E. B. White holler uncle and—in the wings, waiting to come on—are ten more paragraphs of same. But we know this is a bit much to force-feed the reader. His interest will wander elsewhere. So we tell the color of her eyes, rave about the tattoo on her arm, describe how she yearns for Rock Hudson, and then, add this:

> "Not really Rock Hudson," Hilda told herself. "But certainly not Herbert. There are men and there are men!"
> Hilda stopped to consider this thought. She wanted to be fair.
> "On second thought," she decided, "Herbert isn't really much of a man. He has false teeth, wears a rug,and. . ."
> Hilda, though she didn't know it, was too much of a dreamer for her own—and anyone else's—good. She. . .

Thus, the tedium broken by dialogue, we trot out more paragraphs of description. The dialogue we inserted moves the plot along, keeps the reader reading, and adds lines which were not there before. To fill two hundred pages, don't look gift horses in the mouth. Any time you see a mouth, put words in it. Make it speak. Purists will note that Hilda's chatter is not actually dialogue. She is talking with no one. That's a monologue, they are quick to say. Guess again. That's more of a soliloquy, but rather than learn a word a day, let's call all speeches dialogue. Okay? This book isn't that formal.

A Two-Way Street

Dialogue is not hard to write if you pay attention to the everyday world and make your dialogue sound real. For instance, don't let one character speak for pages at a time. Real life is not that way. When was the last time anyone let you say more than five sentences before you were interrupted? Unless the boss is delivering his Christmas speech or the lawyer is reading the will, some dunderhead is bound to pop up and say:

"Yes. That's what happened all right. I remember because. . ."
Or:
"That reminds me of the time when. . ."
Or:
"Your wife says it happened different. *She* says. . ."
Long speeches in novels are simply long paragraphs that are set off with quotation marks. We don't like long speeches in real life so why

should we like them in novels? Conversation is give-and-take. That's what dialogue is all about. Eavesdrop on actual conversations. Listen to that guy and that girl on the bus. Before she can complete a sentence, he dives in with a new thought or, at least, a qualification on the present one. If this is the way people talk in real life, and it is, shouldn't they talk this way in your novel, too?

The problem is in the *writing* of dialogue. We usually write better English than we speak. Our sentences have subjects and predicates. Thus, when we first attempt dialogue, we fall into a trap. We make people speak as they would write. We end up not with a conversation but written messages talked back and forth. I submit in all kindness: President Eisenhower. His written communications were simple and efficient. But did you ever hear him speak off the cuff? His sentences got lost, they turned strange corners, and they rambled on and on, throwing syntax to the wind. Allow your characters the same quality.

However. To ramble every which way in real life is one thing; to ramble (ineffeciently and unedited) in your novel is another, Keep your dialogue efficient. Edit, edit, edit. Throw out each speech that needn't be said. Throw out each sentence. Throw out each word.

"Ah!" is better than *"Well, how about that!"*
"Wait!" is better than *"Wait a minute!"*
"I love you" is better than *"I love you very much."*
"See?" is better than *"Do you see?"*

One is how real people talk. The other is how, if they could write their conversations, they would talk.

Do this: next time you tackle dialogue, forget the *he saids, she saids,* how her eyes narrowed, how his voice trembled, and whether the sun was going up, down, or sideways. To see if your dialogue reads the way dialogue should, write what they say as if you were writing a play.

He: Wait?
She: Ah?
He: I love you.
She: Big deal!

Before you send your novel to market, of course, add the rest, which turns your dialogue into—perhaps—a scene like this:

> When he entered the room, he saw Hilda. She stood, teetering on the window ledge, eighty stories up. She seemed excited about something.
>
> "Wait!" he said.
>
> He could see what troubled her. To jump or not to jump. She had always been indecisive.
>
> "Ah?" she said.
>
> He had to stop her, but if he moved near, zap! out she would go. He decided to reach her with words.
>
> "I love you," he said.
>
> "Big deal!" she said—and jumped.

My point, poorly made, is that dialogue must sound the way people talk. Sometimes we have to scrape off the rest of our writing to see if our dialogue holds true. Sidney Carton's speech about "being a far better thing I do than I have ever done" went out with button shoes. Hilda, teetering on the window sill, has no time for second-act curtain speeches. After you write your dialogue, read it aloud and hear how it sounds. Or, write it as we did above, in play form. Best, if you have a tape recorder handy, record your dialogue. Even though you're not the world's greatest actor you might be surprised when you "hear" your dialogue played back. Just reading your dialogue aloud will tell you if the speech is—or isn't—natural.

How do you develop an ear for dialogue? Eavesdrop, as I suggested. As you wander about town, eavesdrop, eavesdrop, eavesdrop. Collect speech patterns like:

"And I said to her. . .and she said to me. . .and I said to her. . ."
Note: I did not use *sez* which, although apt, is harder to read than *says* or *said*.

Let your characters speak as real people do. Your readers are real, aren't they? Well, anything that brings the reader and your characters closer together helps hold the reader to the end of your novel. Three cheers for empathy! Let the reader be able to say:

"Yes. That's how things are."
Or, if you have another kind of reader, let him be able to say:
"Yep. That's how she goes."

Is This Dialect Necessary?

Which brings us to the treacherous subject of dialects. This subject should be subtitled "How Cute Can A Novelist Get!" A little dialect goes a long way—and usually too far. Writers who delight in writing dialects defend their cuteness by saying:

"But that's how people talk. I want to capture the flavor of these people."

My answer is:

"Who are you kidding? People might sound that way to you but to them, you sound funny too. They don't have the dialect, you do."

Do you believe as I do—that if people try to communicate coherently (and they all do) then we as writers should try to communicate coherently, too? The real people we meet each day are not trying to entertain us with dialect. Certainly they're not trying to sound quaint. They are trying to *say* something. Which is more important, to write funny dialect or let your readers in on what your characters are talking about? Besides, dialects are hard to write and harder to read. Writing dialect is an art which, once mastered, should not be practiced. To write a dialect is to write phonetically the speech pattern of the hillbilly, cowboy, Maine lobsterman, or Aunt Widebottom. To write phonetically is to write gibberish. *If* might become *ef* and in extreme cases *effen*. But *if* is easier to read. When the southern lass speaks, *I* becomes *Ah,* but you'll not convince her of that; she thinks she's saying *I*. Fonetiks giv us the rong noshuns uhbowt the wa pepul tok, wooden u sa? If you must write dialect, go ahead. Only do this: when you submit your script to market, include English subtitles. Most dialects are as ridiculous as baby talk. Just as baby talk is rough on babies, dialects are hard on readers. What baby learned proper English hearing only *itchee coo?*

Stick with English and don't show off. Foreign language in a novel is a wasted exercise in vanity. *Pardonnez-moi* should read *pardon me* and what's wrong with *please* in place of *s'il vous plait?* I know these words because I studied French in high school. But if your reader studied Latin you've left him out in left field, a dirty trick to play on a guy who shelled out money for your book.

Let your reader know who says what. Nothing exasperates more than dialogue in which the reader loses his way. *He saids* and *she saids* are essential. You may not need them with every speech, but when in doubt, use them. Otherwise the luckless reader will run into something like this:

> "Hilda, I love you," he said.
> "Do you, Herbert?" she said.
> "Yes!"
> "Are you certain you love me?"
> "Why? Don't you love me?"
> "I love you."
> "You do?"
> "I'll always love you."
> "I'll always love you."
> "I'm so happy."
> "Me, too."

Quickly! Who spoke last—Hilda or Herbert? Avoid this confusion two ways:

> "Hilda, I love you," he said.
> "Do you, Herbert?" she said.
> "Yes!"
> "Are you certain you love me?" she said.
> "Why? Don't you love me?"
> "I love you," she said.
> "You do?" he said.
> "I'll always love you."
> "I'll always love you," he said.
> "I'm so happy," she said.
> "Me, too."

And so is the reader. The second way to avoid the confusion is to use their names.

> "Hilda, I love you."
> Do you, Herbert?"
> "Yes!"
> "Herbert, are you certain you love me?"
> "Why, Hilda? Don't you love me?"
> "I love you."
> "Hilda, you do?"
> "Herbert, I'll always love you."

"I'll always love you, Hilda."
"I'm so happy."
"Me, too."

Either way lets the reader know who is talking. Notice, though, I used *said* throughout. Some writers, wishing to show how many words they know, avoid *said*. Their characters go six ways from Sunday to keep from *saying* anything. Instead the characters utter

breathe
state
declare
assert
aver
allege
remark
comment
observe
note
mention
murmur
mutter
mumble
sigh
gasp
whisper
pant
exclaim
yell
cry
bark
yelp
yip
growl
snap
snarl
hiss

thunder
boom
scream
grunt
snort
roar
bellow
bawl
shriek
screech
squeal
whine
wail
prate
prattle
babble
jabber
gibber
blather
spout
gush
jaw
gas
converse
counsel
discuss
refer and recite words at each other. So much fancy footwork! There sits *said,* one of the nicest and hardest-working words in a writer's vocabulary. *Said* dosen't get in the way. Other words can. For example:

"Hilda," he murmured, "I love you."
"Do you, Herbert?" she breathed.
"Yes!" he thundered.
"Are you certain you love me?" she whined.
"Why?" he gasped. "Don't you love me?"
"I love you," she yelled.

"You do?" he hissed.
"I'll always love you," she mentioned.
"I'll always love you," he alleged.
"I'm so happy," she whimpered.
"Me, too," he panted.

The words are nice and, used sparingly, add to your novel. But, if every time you turn around, you use another word for *said,* your reader will become more aware of your vocabulary than your plot. Let's be reasonable. He's not reading to see a writer work. He reads to be entertained.

"But," you say, "sometimes *said* isn't enough. *Said* doesn't tell *how* the character said anything."

True, but I still insist *said* is better than *sighed.* In most instances, that is. Anyway, if you must amplify a word, especially the word *said,* avoid adverbs at all cost, especially those Tom Swifties: she said gladly, she said sadly, she said merrily, he said hungrily, she said icily, he said hotly. Strike out every adverb you can. Adverbs are the most useless words in the English language.

"Big deal!" you say smugly, grimly, and indignantly. "How can you modify *said* which is a verb unless you use an adverb?"

Easy as pie. Change *"I love you," she said sadly.* to *"I love you," she said. Her voice was sad.* Which gets the message across better? The first way, *sad* is only an afterthought, a weak tagalong. The second way, *sad* has the importance it deserves. Or, if *sad* is not important, kill the adverb *sadly* and go about your business; the word had no business there in the first place.

There are times when *said* won't do.

"I hate you!" she shouted. is better than *"I hate you!" she said. Her voice was loud.* On the other hand, *"I hate you!" she said. Her voice was loud.* is better than *"I hate you!" she said loudly. Shout,* in this case, is better than *said.*

So you see there are times when even the nicest rules must be broken, but let the exceptions be few and far between. If ever you are going to be indiscreet, as the poet said, be indiscreet discreetly.

Chapter 5

Where Does Your Novel Happen?

Where does your novel *happen*—down the street or in Saudi Arabia? In other words, what is the setting? Against what geographical backdrop do your characters kiss?

I don't know about you, but I write about what I know and suggest that you do the same. Write only about Saudi Arabia if Saudi Arabia is a bus-ride away. But if down the street is a Maine fishing village, let that village be your setting. If Topeka, Kansas, is what you see through your picture window, fine and dandy. Use Topeka as your setting. If you're in Vermont, Wisconsin, North Carolina, or Texas, what's wrong with the settings there?

If you've not lived among the New Britain aborigines don't write a South Pacific stem-winder based on blow-gun hunters. You might have the natives yammering the wrong dialect. Your novel needs a setting, but use a setting you know about. Leave the Lapalmanians, if those blow-gun hunters are called that, to the Lapalmanians, and concentrate instead on where you are or where you were. How can anyone write about a geographic area he knows so little about? With settings, which is the reason for this chapter, this is particularly true. Get that faraway look out of your eyes. Look out the kitchen window instead.

Some novelists on their first trip to the typewriter recall dashing novels of yore. These writers see visions of husky men fight life-and-death struggles in the frozen tundra, heroes stagger across deserts, or Quasimodo do headstands on the cathedral. These visions have many Grand Settings: jungles, oceans, Trafalgar Square, plus more castles than you'd care to heat in a million years. If these visions are Americanized, the settings are the White House, Atlanta burning (from the movie *Gone With The Wind*), Chicago, New York, Hollywood, and upon occasion, Niagra Falls. Swell visions all! This, the writer shouts, is the stuff that Great Novels are made of.

My only advice to such writers is, cool it.

Visions are nice places to visit but do you want your characters to live there? For one thing, what do you really know about the White House? And were you there when Atlanta burned? Or were you at the popcorn machine, feeding your face? If you choose to write about the inner workings of Hollywood, where do you get your information: from a movie magazine or was your mother a star? When did you last pot around in a jungle or cross a desert? Been to the frozen north lately? Buckingham Palace is a fine setting, but only if you know whereof you speak. And if you do know that heap intimately, why are you writing fiction? Write about the royal family. Everyone else there does. Put your visions away and be practical.

I have the vague feeling you know more about buying a used car than walking a high-wire or fixing the plumbing of an Atlas booster. If you're a circus performer or a space plumber, forgive me. It's the rest of us I'm talking to.

"Listen," you say. "Great novels need great settings—and what's so great about a used-car lot?"

Agreed. For now, at least. The used-car lot setting—or any other setting: kitchen, drug store, shopping center, main street, or pizza parlor —is ordinary, isn't it? Face facts. Until you—and you alone—do something wonderful with words to such places, these settings are going to stay ordinary. Only you can bring them to life on the printed page. Will you admit that you are better equipped to describe a used-car lot than you are equipped to describe the men's room at Buckingham Palace? The used-car lot is handy. Buckingham Palace is not. You, the used-car lot, and your readers have much in common. And anything that can bring you and the reader closer together isn't all bad.

A later chapter shows you how to make the used-car lot sing—if you put your mind to the task, that is. To write drama into the *Titanic's* misadventure is easy. To make a used-car lot dramatic is not. But who said writing a novel was child's play? Take my word for it. If you can make your settings come alive, such settings will have new meaning to your readers. You will have turned the ordinary into art. But stick with the canvasses you know. You can paint a picture of the used-car lot quicker than you can paint the *Titanic* sinking. You don't have to research the used-car lot. You do the *Titanic*. Did the passengers use Zippo lighters? How long were the ladies' dresses then? Did the state rooms have florescent lights—or which? Aren't you glad the used-car lot is just downtown, waiting to be looked at?

Your Personal Vision

If you hail from the farm, you already have plenty of private visions to conjure up for your typewriter. The same is true if you hail from the slums, subdivisions, or the piney forests of the south. These are special visions that only *you* have seen through your eyes and heart. Only *you* can write them. Only *you* can recreate the settings of your childhood and your settings of now. Write of these wonderful things only *you* know. No matter how shabby, clean, or ornate your childhood neighborhood was, the setting will have more meaning to you than the neighborhood of any other child. Use your childhood settings as your vision. Use the street you first drove your father's car along. Use the church where you were married. Use the gloomy apartment where your grandparents now sit as prisoners. You don't need the Sahara Desert. Refuse delivery on the Atlantic Ocean. Send the Swiss Alps back. You have more personal visions in you than you will ever be able to put down on paper.

If Walt Whitman could hear America singing we can hum some of its tunes. Give value to the ordinary and give magic to the mundane. Danger today is not a dragon that snorts fire. Danger today is our illogical love of complexities. We insist on making life more complicated than life is. We bypass, ignore, or take for granted simple pleasures. We race here and there, join thousands of clubs, attend thousands of meetings, and yet, when evening comes and we go home, we fail to see the beauty of our street or to find solace in our homes. The dreariest flat in the dreariest flat building possesses at least some beauty, but who will point this beauty out? I know, I know. An angry writer, properly steamed, can turn a wedding into farce and make angry fun of the bride. But I happen not to be an angry writer. I happen to seek beauty and solace, not ugliness and frustration. So if you wish to write a bitter novel that will make your readers sad and lonely, do the opposite of everything I suggest. Instead of finding heaven in hell, find hell in heaven. Whichever route you follow, though, find good *or* bad in the settings you *know*. The canals of Venice may smell foul because the canals are open sewers filled with garbage, but I'm not sure of this. I've not been there. On the other hand, I do know the way the back alleys of Negro ghettos smell. So I'll not write of Venice. I'll write of Negro children forced to play among the broken glass. I'll not write in anger. I'll paint that setting with words that are honest. My words will note not only the ugliness that exists, but my words will find beauty in the noise that children make.

Do the world a favor. Cynics will make fun of you, but seek beauty in each setting. I don't suggest that everything—*everywhere*—is coming up roses. But roses do exist, if only as magazine pictures that first-graders paste on tenement walls.

Give your novel everyday settings, then with your writing make those settings more. Note beauty where none has been noted before. Thus, by reading your novel, readers will know beauty, too. True, such stuff as I write and you might write will not shake the world or cause nations to topple. But then I'm not a world-shaking nation-toppler of a writer and I've no intention of becoming one.

Whatever *your* intentions, employ settings that you know intimately. This rule might eliminate Buckingham Palace, of course, as well as the White House and many other places including, we trust, federal prisons.

Don't let your settings overpower the plot, though. Don't let your setting, through description that pulls out all stops, get in the way of your novel's basic task: to tell a story. Settings, however nice, are not that nice. If you're writing a novel, don't write a travelogue.

Recheck Your Setting

Don't trust your memory. When you describe a city you once knew well, revisit it first if you can, and look around. The years might have made your recollection of the setting as unreal and illogical as the true tales oldtimers make up. Try to revisit the scenes of your novel's action to see if the things you said happened could have happened there. Hilda, as a child, jumped that creek? Look again. If she had ever jumped across *that* creek, pal, you could have entered her in the Olympics. Whatever actual settings your novel contains, someone—usually a well-meaning wiseacre—will look at that setting with your novel's action in mind. You inspect the site first. Don't let Hilda do the impossible.

In rechecking your settings check trivia that might, if incorrect, stand out like a sore thumb. Did they, in those days, have dial telephones? Did streetcars travel that street, or did busses? That shopping center is there now but was—or wasn't—it there then? Can the sun set behind the brewery as your novel says it can, or did you remember wrong? Is the skyscraper that high and were the curbs that high? Were saloons open or was Prohibition throughout the land? Trivia, trivia, trivia, but know this: recreate the most beautiful street, but if it runs north and south in your novel, and east and west in real life, a reader will question everything else in your novel, too. And he will be right as rain to do it.

Don't guess. Check the telephone company. They're a cheerful lot who will bend over backwards to keep your novel accurate. Check the city transit company. They're cheerful too, until you hand the driver a ten spot in the rush hour. Check city hall. Check the newspaper files. Whatever you do, don't check that old geezer leaning against the fence. History might flow through his veins, but his circulation could be whopperjawed. His memory may be no better than yours and might be even worse. Write to the town if you can't visit it. Or, a few long-distance telephone calls can quickly supply the facts you need.

Example: in a novel I once wanted to rub out a character and for once, I was taking my own advice: I tried to kill him in a more original way than hurling him off a bridge. I had him climb one of those high towers that carry electricity from city to city. Only after I got him up there, I wasn't certain of what happened next. What did he have to touch? And what would happen when he did? Would he, like a penny in a fuse box, make a city dark? Also, I had seen birds land on these high-voltage lines, sit around, tweet, and fly away refreshed. Why don't birds get killed? I felt that if I wondered, a reader would wonder, too. I called the electric company, asked the nice lady how to kill a man on one of her towers, and also, why birds didn't die. She turned me quickly over to the engineering department which solved my problem fast. Birds don't die because they don't touch anything that would complete a high-voltage circuit—zap!—through their dinky bodies. A city would not go dark because when one circuit fails, bypass circuitry takes over. This, of course, was before the Manhattan power outage. As for killing my character up there, the engineers said that although they didn't like to use the towers for things like that (they mentioned something about public relations), they would look into the matter for me. Good old utility company! In ten minutes I had every answer. My point here is, whatever information your novel requires, that information is usually available.

Need a factory setting? Take a factory tour. Same goes for museums, bakeries, newspaper offices, and funeral homes. But caution: with tours you only scratch the surface. So for goodness sake, if you must put your character into a factory setting that you have only toured briefly, don't go overboard on that part of his life. In such cases, be clever. *Suggest* the setting. Don't go all out. No one is that clever. The same holds true for geographic settings you yourself have not visited. Suppose our Hilda takes her vacation in London. You've not been there. Well, whatever you do, don't *you* describe her in that setting, let Hilda *herself* talk about it. And even then, ride herd on her. Don't let her get carried away. But *how* can she talk about it? Easy. If you read *National Geographic* magazine you can put the right words in her mouth. The June 1966 issue, for example, offers an article called *"One Man's London"* by Allan C. Fischer, Jr. Read the picture captions and have Hilda say:

"The telephone building over there doesn't have gadgets on its roof like ours does here. The gadgets are around the tower's middle, of all places!"

Or, use the map of London that same issue contained:

> "Honest to Pete, I just had to walk along Birdcage Walk. Never again though. You know how I go ape over canaries. Well, I started at Buckingham Palace and got clear to Whitehall without seeing a single bird cage!"

Or:

> "Some parts of London look like Chicago. I mean, what's the use of going clear over there to see something we got here at home? Everyone raved so about Alton. Well, I went and looked. Nothing but apartment buildings I could have seen anywhere. Not Englishy at all!"

Or:

> "But Hillsleigh Road was cute. That's out in Kennsington. Row houses, same as Society Hill in Philly. Cute, but terribly oldish and terribly expensivish."

The same issue of the *National Geographic* could have taken our friend to the castles along the Loire River, but you know Hilda. She would have considered them *Europish*, which means it's high time we looked into this business of description. What's the good of a setting if you can't describe it?

And words like *Englishy* won't do.

Chapter 6

Description in Small Doses

Never, never, never lay description on too thick.

Your novel should have only enough description to let your reader see, feel, hear, taste, smell, and—if need be—touch. For description to accomplish all that could mean you might end up with a lot of words. Guess again. One paragraph of description is better than a dozen, one sentence is better than a paragraph, and one word is better than a sentence. Pages of description are tedious. So is one word too much.

The question is, how completely should a restaurant, street, or hotel room be described? Let common sense prevail. If Hilda and Herbert are kissing in a public telephone booth, why describe the booth's size or tell how, when the door opens and shuts, the light goes off and on? We have all seen a public telephone booth, we know what you're talking about, so don't belabor the obvious. Don't say the booth is cramped, don't describe the dial system, and don't sing the praises of A. T. & T. for creating public smooching headquarters. Tell your characters to kiss, read the dirty words scribbled on the wall, and get out.

"Wait!" you say. "I have a particular *feeling* about public telephone booths. I could rave for hours about them. They. . ."

Rave on your own time. Don't waste the reader's time. He wants to read a novel, not a love letter to the telephone company. Perhaps the company just disconnected his telephone for an unpaid bill. He might not feel the way you do—and you will have lost a friend. You'll lose enough friends with your novel without going out of your way to alienate strangers. *Don't describe what doesn't need describing.* That's the secret of description. Every chance you get to use description, don't.

Skip the Unnecessary

Think of the many things some writers describe that waste everyone else's time. One is the ring of the telephone. Why say it rings *persistently?* It rings—period. If it rings intermittently you have something, and that something better be a telephone repair man. Unless you're a music student with perfect pitch, why describe a dial tone? Unless they play *Yankee Doodle,* why describe the door chimes? Unless it has no wheels, why describe a Greyhound bus? Why describe typewriters, scrambled eggs, door knobs, record players, revolving doors, ping pong balls, the bunnyhop, or a canary's tweet? Make up a list of items that don't need describing and then, don't describe them. If you *must* describe something, describe the shape of a football or Coke bottle. You'll end up saying, "To hell with that noise. Everyone *knows* what they look like!" My point exactly. Everyone knows what a telephone booth looks like, too. Why waste your time and the reader's describing it?

There! In one fell swoop we have eliminated a lot of writing for you. But facing us are items that *do* need describing. True, hotel chains like Holiday Inn make life easier on poor writers because every room in every inn is the same as every other, but generally, other hotel rooms can be anywhere between lavish and sleazy. They can smell of fresh air (from a spray can) or disinfectant (from another spray can). The view from the hotel window can be Times Square, Lake Michigan, the Atlantic Ocean, the Golden Gate Bridge, or an air shaft, sheet metal plant, super highway, *or*—if one is lucky—the YWCA sundeck. Rooms can cost from fifty cents to fifty dollars a night. The difference is maid service, clean sheets, and chicken wire.

When you park your characters in a hotel room, let the reader know if they're at the Ritz or the flophouse. A few quick sentences give your reader the flavor of that room.

> The room was small. The floors creaked. The window was covered with grime. To turn out the light did not create darkness. The *DRINK COCA COLA* sign outside never turned off.

Better yet, let your characters describe the room. This permits your reader to know more about them and the room at the same time.

> "Herbert," she said, "I've never seen a place so swell. Look. There's the dump where pa works."
> Herbert tested the bed. Its lack of mattress annoyed him.
> "It certainly isn't the Ritz," he said. "The manager didn't send fruit. The bellhop didn't hang our things in the closet."
> "There ain't no closets," she said. "But smell that beautiful smell. Lilacs?"
> "Airwick," he said.

There's another method you might *not* buy: attach meanings to things which have no meanings. To describe the flophouse that way, put more spin on your description and treat the room as a living thing with personality. Use adjectives usually reserved for people.

> Their hotel room had lost its youth. Its floors creaked with middleage. It had not bathed in years. Grime covered its windows. All night the *DRINK COCA COLA* sign looked in and made fun. If rooms could cry, this one had earned the right.

Why do this? Because description must be more than tired adjectives thrown at the reader. Contrast is the best way to describe things. Describe a house as a house and your description is ordinary as rain. But describe a house as a person who experiences hope, happiness, sadness, and pain—and your reader will take notice. The reverse is true. Give people the adjectives usually reserved for houses, streets, and even insects. Thus:

> She was, to children, a haunted house they dare not visit.

Or:

> Everyone else was an expressway, racing somewhere, full of purpose; she was a street labeled dead end.

Or:

> She was a wobbly spider of a woman who had spun a rainy lifetime of broken webs.

Kill Those Cliche's

Avoid bromides that readers look at but don't see at all. You've heard old-time politicians speak. They love phrases like *"from the sunny slopes of California to the rockbound coasts of Maine."* To a politician of the old school all opponents are *"esteemed opponents,"* all soldiers are *"our fighting boys,"* and when *"our fighting boys"* get hurt, they don't get hurt but they *"shed—or spill—their blood."* Bromides can be your novel's death rattle. Study each adjective and adverb with care. Readers are used to *bores* being *crashing bores,* so take another look at that bore of yours. Make him a *round-the-clock bore,* or a *professional bore who lost his amateur standing when he learned to talk.* If you persist in using bromides, dress them up.

"Herbert," she said," could bore the socks off an elephant."

Don't fret. All of us use bromides. Some of us just try to find them before an editor does. We are forever writing of *deep* forests, *bustling* crowds, *driving* rain, *angry* mobs, *twinkling* stars, *ribbons of cement* (meaning, of course, highways), *steep* stairs, *stuffy* rooms, the *lateness* of the hour, *fresh* eggs, and *resounding* crashes. Distrust every adjective the second time around. *Deep* forests? To *walk into a forest* reads faster—and better—than *to walk into a deep forest.* Anyway, who ever heard of a *shallow* forest? *Bustling* crowds? What does that mean? *Driving* rain? Perhaps. But why not just *rain?* If the wind is blowing, fine. Wind drives the rain. Say so. Which is better: to be *out in a driving rain* or *out in the wind and rain?* *Angry* mobs? Show me a mob that isn't angry and I'll show you a mob that isn't there. *Twinkling* stars? Do all stars twinkle and if they do, doesn't the phrase nauseate you? *Ribbons of concrete* has been so overworked readers read it without reading it, and if that's how readers react to fancy prose, call it a highway. *Steep* stairs? The degree of steepness means nothing. Eighty steps wind me; eight steps don't. *Stuffy* rooms mean nothing. Be specific. What makes the room stuffy: dust, drapes, or dirty socks? *Lateness* of the hour? Wasted words. Give the correct time. What's late for you might be early for me. *Fresh* eggs? Wasted adjective. All eggs are presumed fresh. When your character finds a *stale* one, say so. And if a crash doesn't *resound* it's not much of a crash. Okay, okay, okay. Write your bromides—you will anyway; then edit them out.

Your fifth grade teacher might quarrel with this next premise of mine, but to me a sentence should do one thing only. Why make sentences more complicated than they are? A sentence should describe action or describe an object; it shouldn't do both. A sentence that tries to go two directions at once weakens one of its directions. I'd better explain fast. I believe *She entered the weatherbeaten old three-story house* is not as effective as *She entered the house. It was three stories high, weatherbeaten and old.*

Perhaps to you the sentences are identical, but not to me. The first one says she enters the house and, in addition, tells us what shape the house is in. To me, if the fact that the house is three stories high, weatherbeaten and old is important enough to write, such description should not be in a sentence that says something else. On the other hand, if the house being weatherbeaten *et al* is not important, why write it anywhere? Besides I don't approve of nouns that are littered with adjectives. The second sentence employs the same adjectives, but there, at least, they earn their keep. In the first sentence they got in the way, made hash of a simple thought, and there you are. You see how fussy I am? To me, too many adjectives—one after the other—defeat their own purpose. Let each adjective have value unto itself. Don't let it get lost in a crowd. If an adjective is important, make the reader aware of it. If an adjective is not important, get rid of it.

Forget style. Let style happen—as it should—*naturally*. Style is *not* the clever use of words any more than style is lipstick on a girl's lips. Style is what's inside the words and the heart of the lipstick wearer. Keep your descriptions simple. Don't doll them up with rouge and false eyelashes. When a girl overloads her face she is saying real beauty does not exist. When you doll up a sentence with a long, long string of adjectives, you're saying the sentence is mute without them. You're saying the sentence can't carry its own weight. Better to use one apt adjective than a string of them that takes up space. One beauty mark adds charm to a pretty girl. Too many and you think she's catching something.

A New Way to Use the Thesaurus

In another chapter we saw how to find different ways to say "anger." We used the thesaurus. There is another way, not listed by its authors, to use the thesaurus. Your thesaurus can be used to trigger not only new words, but whole new thoughts and whole new sentences. In fact. you and your thesaurus can have private brain-storming sessions the way advertising agencies do. Ain't that grand? Suppose you want to describe a tattered house. You could, by the regular way, look up in your thesaurus words like *old, rundown, weathered,* and *dilapidated.* Or, you can do this, which takes a little longer. Clear your mind of everything but how to describe the house, open your thesaurus to the index, and read straight down the entire list of words. Don't skip a single one. If a word strikes your fancy, pause. Or, if it doesn't, pass on. Let's try it.

Aaronic. "No thanks! Don't even know what it means."

Aaron's rod. "I'm still out in left field. This is a stupid system."

Abacist. "Nope."

Abaction. "Never heard of that, either."

Abactor. "Still lost. This is a waste of time."

Abacus. "Yeah, the Chinese use them for—hold a minute. An abacus works with clicking noises, doesn't it? And the word sounds scary and antique. Let's see. Suppose I said, 'When the storm came, the house's venetian blinds blow with clickety-clicks, each venetian blind an abacus that adds days and years. . .' I'll jot that sentence down. Might use it. Better get on or I'll be here all night."

Abaddon. "Means devil, or hell, or something like that, doesn't it? Could the devil be working the venetian blinds? Ah, there's a good phrase: the devil wind! I'll jot that down, too. If I hadn't stumbled across abaddon I'd not have it."

Abaff, abaft. "Certainly nothing there."

Abaliente. "Wonder what that means, if anything?"

Abandon. "I'd forgotten that word! Maybe I have something here. *The house that time abandoned.* Or, what about *the house that time forgot?* Let's look under the verbs in the subclassification of *abandon . . .*"

Perhaps. I'll list it for luck."

Leave undone. "There's a thought. *Time left nothing undone: it made the house sag, filled the yard with weeds, chipped the paint. . .* Perhaps. I'll list it for luck."

Forsake. "Hey, even better! *The house stood forsaken. . .* Good. Now I'm getting somewhere."

Break a habit. "Huh? Not sure. How about: *It was an old house filled with old habits—floors that sagged, doors that creaked . . .?"*

Disuse. "Perhaps, but *forsake* is better."

Discard. "This word might work. *The house was an antique discard on a street filled with modern split-levels. . . ."*

Relinquish. "I could say *It has relinquished its right to happiness."*

Swear off. "Whee! *It could not swear off its yesterdays . . ."*

Well, here we are halfway through one column of one page of my thesaurus, but consider what we have accomplished:

> The house stood forsaken. It had relinquished its right to happiness. It was too filled with memories and strange noises to swear off its yesterdays. So there it stood, an antique discard in a split-level neighborhood, a house that time forgot.

I'll be the first to admit that the description of the house is not the greatest, but that description is more apt than anything I've written thus far about the place. And remember, I used only one half of one column of one page in my thesaurus. Each page has four columns of words which means I used only one-eighth of one page—and my thesaurus index has nearly six hundred pages.

Had I spent more time scanning the index I could have come up with a description of that house that would have knocked your eye out. You could have, too. But if we had stared into space waiting for the *"right word"* we might still have been staring. Use time efficiently. Every minute must count. Don't waste time waiting for inspiration. Inspire yourself. Let your thesaurus help you.

Now comes the sad part. It isn't too sad, of course, but let's pretend that paragraph which describes the house is the best we can do, but also that the paragraph is too long. Let's throw some gems away. Didn't we suggest at the start of this chapter that one paragraph is better than many, that one sentence is better than one paragraph, and that one word is better than one sentence? Let's practice what we preach. First, let's reduce that paragraph to one sentence and see what happens.

What usually happens is, the first time around we are reluctant to throw out any gems—so we end up with a whopper of a sentence like this:

> Forsaken, forgotten, with only split-levels for friends, the house was an antique too filled with memories and strange noises to be anything more than a discard that time forgot.

Whew! Long, complicated, confusing! Says too much, doesn't it? Far too many thoughts. Let's try again. Good-by, gems!

> Forsaken among split-levels, the house—antique—was a discard that time forgot.

Brief, but not much better. Gone is the "filled with memories and strange noises." Gone is the "swearing off its yesteryears" which we didn't use at all. But at least we have the start of a sentence that will not slow the plot. Let's take another crack at it, adding whatever new thoughts the old ones might have triggered. And, also, let's keep it simple.

> Time forgot it. Split-levels ignored it. The house was a rummage-sale discard no one would cart away.

Better still:

> The house was a rummage-sale discard no one would cart away.

Or:

> The house was a rummage-sale discard waiting for time to cart it away.

Or:

> "Herbert, that spooky house gives me the willies."

Or:

Chapter 7

Four Ways to Put Pizzazz in Your Novel

There's a television commercial about a tooth paste that does more than make your choppers white. The man says:

"It puts *pizzazz* in your smile."

Let's put *pizzazz* in your novel. We'll say your characters are well-drawn from real life, your plot has no wasted motion, your dialogue sings an efficient song, but there the pages sit. Somehow, suddenly, your novel doesn't seem as brilliant as it might be. What to do! You've written about ordinary people. You can't make them do extraordinary things. That would not be cricket. Besides, it wouldn't be believable. Also, it would be cheating. Clark Kent may work wonders in a telephone booth but the rest of us make telephone calls there. How can you —without junking your plot, bringing in a new cast of characters, and starting over—put *pizzazz* in your novel?

First review the plight of your characters and while you're doing that, shed tears for you and me. What makes your novel drag is what makes the real world drag. Although we don't intend our lives that way, we live lives as ordinary as old shoes. We don't win raffles, movie stars don't know we exist, and the only time the cop calls is to peddle tickets to the policemen's ball. The only excitement we get is a wrong number in the middle of the night. Poor, ordinary, uncomplicated us! Are we the kind they make movies about? Even Walt Disney gives us a wide berth; we have one too many fingers. Are we the kind they write plays about? No. If we were Edward Albee characters our spouses would sue for divorce. If we were the free spirits that William Saroyan creates, our bosses would fire us and children would throw stones. If we were the fragile wisps of moon fluff that Tennessee Williams says we are, daylight would make us vanish. Ian Fleming had James Bond. We have the butcher who hates us. Simply put, we are not the characters upon which novels are built and when we are, the novels bog. Sad. Real sad.

Yet your novel, which is about people you know, has no other kind of people to offer. No one you know has robbed a bank, scaled the Alps, or lifted off to the moon. You're writing about people as ordinary as yourself which forces them to be bland. Question is, can you pump life into these bland paper characters who all put on their pants the same?

Sure thing!

Consider first the plight of the mystery writer. When he dreams up a new way to create death half of his problems are solved. Shooting bullets at people has become a bore. Sticking knives into them is old hat. And poison is distasteful as well as no fun. The mystery writer faces an awful problem of technology. Why should murder be a Dark Ages' pastime when, all around, science leaps forward like a jack rabbit. The mystery writer seeks new ways to do old deeds. What of the kitchen disposal, perhaps, to get rid of the *corpus delecti?* The simpler days of tying victims to railroad tracks have gone. With train service so poor these days, the victim might be tied there for days before a train came along. So much for the art of murder. The point is, ordinary murderers don't get written about. Imagination is the key to the mystery novel.

Well, if imagination is the key to the art of murder, can't we apply that same key to the art of the everyday? Can't you find a different way for your characters to do the ordinary things that you and I do? Find it and you've put *pizzazz* into your book. Here are a few places to work this magic.

How To Keep the Ordinary From Looking That Way

Let's make Hilda, for the time being, the typical housewife. She is a charmer, a genius, perfect mother, and the PTA president, and when she goes to church, she sings on key in the choir. Without making her far-fetched and something she isn't, what can we do to jazz her up? Simple. Find a different way for her to accomplish the ordinary, that's what! Let her do her housework in the nude—and sing operatic arias while she does. Let her paractice welding as a hobby. Let her wish she were a mountain climber, race car driver, Mexican hat dancer, or policewoman. Perhaps because she's fed up with everyone asking what is new, she takes baton twirling on the sly. And wait till they ask her in three weeks! She could, perhaps, run a floating crap game for housewives. Any one of these touches to her character will make her an individual. As the Shadow used to say, "Who knows what evil lurks in the hearts of men?" Go the Shadow one better and say, "Who knows what evil—or anything else for that matter—lurks in the heart of my characters?" Who knows? *You* know. And the rest of us won't know until you tell us.

Let Hilda be the All-American housewife but let her possess secret dreams and urges. Tell us what they are. If you do, she can't be a soap opera character after that. What gal in a soap opera goes secretly to a tattoo artist or slings hash in a French restaurant? Give her foibles. Though we never discuss them with neighbors, we all have our own secret dreams and urges. I've always wanted to break a plate glass window, but if you think I'd mention this on an employment application, think again. We have crazy notions. Let your characters enjoy them too.

Traffic in contrasts. Let the bookkeeper learn karate—not to chop wood but to do damage to his adding machine the day he retires. Let the truck driver have a yen for needlepoint. Contrasts, contrasts, contrasts. Spot these contrasts here and there in your novel. Use them as seasoning. Somtimes ordinary characters with extraordinary habits might create a situation that supplies from the first page to the last a running gag. But don't count on this. In fact, avoid it. Don't be heavy-handed when you treat these facets of your characters. Otherwise Hilda's desire to be a baton twirler and the truck driver's desire to knit will take over—and possibly *change*—your plot.

What you do to set your characters apart from the ordinary you can do to liven your plot. (And more about that in Chapter 12) For instance, instead of your characters dining in an ordinary manner, order a side dish of *pizzazz*. Add the unexpected to the expected.

Characters in Counterpoint

Let's say Hilda and Herbert, dullards who have been married three years, enter a Chinese restaurant. Nothing special about that. This happens every day or we'd have no Chinese restaurants to enter. But let's say, in addition, Hilda wants to tell Henry she wants a divorce. The scene, unless the dialogue is so stunning it knocks our socks off, could be most ordinary, however painful. Counter melody never hurts such a scene. Better to have two things going for you than one. Now, how can we keep the confrontation reasonably sensible, yet still add *pizzazz?* With no attempt at great writing, let's rough it out.

> "There's someting I have to tell you," Hilda said. "Please. Put down the fortune cookie and let me say it my way or..."
>
> "Got a special on egg foo yong," the waiter said.
>
> Hilda drummed her fingers. She wished the waiter would go.
>
> "We'll order later," she said.
>
> "Yes," said Herbert. "Later. It's our anniversary and..."
>
> "You don't like egg foo yong?" said the waiter.
>
> "Later," said Herbert. "We're not ready to order."
>
> "What do you think we're running here," said the waiter, "a Chinese bus stop?"
>
> "Herbert, about us..." Hilda said.
>
> "Lady, I got six tables to wait on..."
>
> "Herbert we're though!" she said. Tears sprang to her eyes. She hadn't meant to tell him this way.
>
> "You mean with this restaurant?" Herbert said. "I agree. Let's go to another and..."
>
> "Okay, so you don't dig egg foo yong," said the waiter. "It's a free country. How about a hot pastrami sandwich..."

...And so on for the rest of the scene. The waiter, a walk-on, plays the buffoon. Herbert has the darndest time understanding what is happening—and the reader feels the frustration Hilda feels. "I remember a pushy waiter once," the reader might recall. Thus, with counter-melody, an ordinary scene becomes extraordinary and the reader gets more for his money. Add *pizzazz* with counter-melody.

One secret of *pizzazz* is to find a different way for your characters to do ordinary things. Suppose Herbert was still courting Hilda. No matter how much meaning a proposal has to its participants, most proposals are ordinary items. To make your proposal scene, which is ordinary, stand out like a sore thumb, put it in a setting that is unlikely. Where? Offhand, Hilda and Herbert could become engaged while they're:

1. trapped between floors in a crowded elevator
2. fighting over chess moves
3. running to catch a bus
4. stuck on a ferris wheel
5. witnesses at a divorce hearing
6. on opposing teams of a debate
7. handcuffed together in a gambling raid
8. dating someone else on a double date
9. shouting because one is accidently locked in a closet
10. giving blood at a blood bank
11. untangling their dogs at a dog-training class
12. waiting in line together at the employment office

All are unlikely—but *ordinary*—settings for the proposal. Make up your own list. Your list will come in handy for just about every scene your novel offers. To make any scene stand out—and have *pizzazz*—let ordinary characters do ordinary things in an extraordinary, but logical, setting. But don't get cute. If your characters are ordinary folk like the rest of us, don't put them in an illogical setting. For instance, to place them in His and Her space ships so they can smooch in outer space is illogical. But to have him making advances in his apartment while watching a capsule's reentry on television *is* logical.

"Herbert! Not now," Hilda said. Her voice was ice. "Wait till splashdown."

Add *pizzazz* still another way. While smooching she might be debating the purchase of shoes—to herself, that is. Men learn these things always after the fact. While he's kissing her he might be wondering if he should put another dime in the parking meter. Touches like these add dimension to your novel. Just don't let them get in the way of your main theme. To have value, counter melody must stay counter melody and *pizzazz* must not get, as the Chinese waiter got, pushy.

Too many offbeat settings, one after the other, rob your characters and plot of basic reality. Your reader will begin to wonder, "Isn't this a bit much'" Hilda might have been proposed to in a stalled elevator but probably that is the only thing that ever happened to her in an unlikely setting. Add *pizzazz*, without using too heavy a hand. Use unlikely settings—the stalled elevator—sparingly. Concentrate on settings like these:

1. home
2. street
3. supermarket
4. movie house
5. high school
6. used-car lot
7. playground
8. city hall
9. amusement park
10. swimming hole

If you want to make such settings vivid, change the time so the setting changes meaning, known becomes unknown, and the ordinary becomes unique. The shopping center going full blast is ordinary. But what of the shopping center at three in the morning? What of the movie house at high noon? Its glamor has fled, its doors stand wide open, sunlight streams in, and dust particles hang suspended. What of a high school corridor during the summer silence? What of the playgound swing at midnight? What of the amusement park in winter? What of busses parked in dark garages? What of steets in the early morning, streets that only cleaning ladies see? If changing the hour of the action from noon to midnight does not add *pizzazz* to your setting, sniff around. Add scents. A familiar whiff that catches a reader by surprise works wonders. You'd be amazed—and alarmed—at the abundance of odors. Mention one or two with each setting. A high school gym, for example, smells of varnish, sweat, and gym shoes. The forest in spring smells of black earth and rotting wood.

To put *pizzazz* in your novel season with the foibles of your characters, juggle settings, tamper with time, and add counter-melody. Only you can prevent forest fires—and only you can prevent your novel from catching fire. Put *pizzazz* in it, every page! *Pizzazz* is more than sex, my friend, so get that look out of you eye.

On second thought, you're coming of age. You've read this far. It is time we talked about the birds, bees, and naked ladies. Send the children from the room. The next chapter concerns itself with you-know-what.

Chapter 8

Is Sex Necessary?

How much sex should your novel contain? There are as many answers to that question as there are writers, readers, censors, and sex maniacs.

You've seen movie ads. Wow! You've rummaged racks of paperbacks. Wow! I can see what you're thinking: to sell your novel you must make it a Sears catalog of sex, a how-to-do-it manual for slow learners. Perhaps. But I doubt it. Anyway, writing a sexy book might please you—or it might shock. My advice is to follow your heart but not necessarily into the bedroom.

A novel that titillates can lay an egg, and, on the other hand, a rousing novel need not arouse. The success of your novel will not depend on the lack or abundance of sex, but upon the quality of your novel itself. You must first make your characters well-rounded, and well-rounded characters do not eat, sleep, and breathe sex every minute of the day. Even Jack the Ripper took coffee breaks.

I know, I know. You'll point to *Candy, Lolita,* and *The One Hundred Dollar Misunderstanding.* Sex, you will say, is the mainstay that made these books bestsellers, so why be a Puritan? Here's why. I suggest that these three books and others like them are novels first, and if they are sex books, sex is way down there on the what-made-it-a-success list. Even novels that feature lesbians, homosexuals, and other charming creatures must contain—other than sex activity—character and plot. And the sex in these novels must be essential to the plot—or out it goes. If to eliminate nonessential words is good, so is to eliminate nonessential romps.

Oh For The Good Old Days Of The Asterisk

In those sweet times, when man and woman got goose-pimples, smooched, and headed for the bedroom, the door closed, asterisks took over, and we waited outside with only our imaginations. Now writers leave nothing to our imaginations. Writers inventory grunts, count pimples, and render the act of love into an act as ordinary as plumbing.

If your plot calls for Hilda and Herbert to make love, I insist that how they go about it is their business, not yours. Beauty is in the eye of the beholder, and so is the impact of a sex scene. Why cheat your reader when he can cheat himself? Let him imagine what he pleases. If you tell him what happens, you face a real problem. If your lovers prove ordinary, some readers will sneer at your old-fashioned ways. If your lovers prove too uninhibited, other readers will report you to the vice squad. You can't win, so why try? Let's all return to the good old days. Lovers loved, there were those asterisks, and plots moved merrily forward.

If you still insist your novel contain sex—not on every other page, I trust—these thoughts might help you. For one thing, a little imagination goes a long way. You can write a whale of a good scene with selected suggestions, without being explicit. For another thing, there are models of good erotic writing on the shelves of nearly every library and in every corner drugstore paperback rack. *Read* some D. H. Lawrence, some Henry Miller. See for yourself how Nabokov handles a delicate situation. Read and compare. Then decide what you think is a skillful handling of the matter and see if you can do as well. Don't go weak with admiration at your first draft. Writing about the most intimate of human relationships is hard to do right, and the line between sexy and ridiculous is a fine one. Keep at it.

While you don't have to write sex scenes based on personal experience, I do suggest you write them with care. Don't presume knowledge. Many girls, now unwed mothers, presumed knowledge. Having the wrong baby is as bad as having the wrong "facts" in your sex scenes. If readers find your characters believable, they might believe your "facts" and end up in hot water. The important thing is, get your facts straight.

Your responsibility as a novelist is not to horse around with mother nature.

When are sex scenes necessary? When you need to show a facet of your characters you can't show any other way. Over-simplified, a sex scene can illustrate that Hilda who is a perfect lady at the PTA is a tigress in bed. The degree of her sex activity can illustrate the degree of her decency or depravity. The intensity—or lack of it—with which she operates could show a side to her character that the committee meeting scene missed completely. Same is true with Herbert. His attitudes toward sex could reveal things about him we'd not learn from seeing him on the golf course. Who dominates? Hilda or Herbert? Who is passive? Are they happy about this? Will their marriage endure? Do they make love only because married people are supposed to, or do they enjoy it and each other? Point is, never describe the sex scene and then let your characters go to sleep. Use this confrontation for character development. They'll be too occupied to think about character development, so, as the author, you'll have to do the thinking for them. In any event, sex scenes must do more than titillate. If that's all the scenes do, write them, get them out of your system, then edit them out of your novel.

Sweet Nothings

The dialogue in a sex scene is only tedious when you make it so. The statement is not as ridiculous as it sounds. Modern man—and woman —is still bothered about sex. Sex is okay to do but not to talk about. Youth is changing this premise—sex is suddenly in the open, body parts are items of small talk—but youth does not write most novels; we middleagers do. We bring to the novel the feeling we learned in the kitchens of our childhood: "Nice" people don't talk about sex. In a few years such attitudes will change, of course, but I am the product as well as the victim of my childhood kitchen. Most lovers are that way, too. Thus, the guy and the girl in novels do not discuss making love. They make love. They have no time to exchange high-falutin' prose. Check some published sex scenes again, and monitor the talk. Sweet nothings? Not likely.

The Coming Of Age Novel

Must every one offer a sex scene? These novels seem to thrive on this amateur horsing. Why not make your novel different? Let the boy or girl discover the magic of reproduction elsewhere. What is so dramatic these days about a teenager losing his—or her—virginity? And before that, what is so dramatic about the first kiss? And before that, if your novel contains such heady stuff, what is so dramatic about the gosh-awful moment these urchins discover the stork didn't bring them? I don't know why every budding novelist feels that sex is the teenager's real trauma. More vital things—these days—preoccupy the teenage brain: pressure from parents to win the right college, the urge to conform to nonconformity, the need to master the electric guitar with its million-dollar amplifier, and making Eagle Scout because Uncle Fuddles did. Frankly, sex is only one of the many traumatic episodes today's teenager will fight his way through. Why attach Great Meanings to items which have no Great Meanings to your young readers? No sex scene you can write can complete with what your kids see in the next car at the drive-in. During this ridiculous period of growing up, love is one thing, but sex is another. Teenagers confuse the two. Let them be confused. Don't you, as a novelist, cater to their confusion. Some of them know more about sex than you or I ever will. Belabor the loss of virginity? Don't waste your time or theirs. A lot of new things are under the sun. A teenager losing his virginity is not one of them. Now, may we return to grown-up sex?

The Great Sex Scene

If you are a male or female, either one, you face a problem when you tackle your Great Sex Scene. A male and a female approach the sex act differently. Man, for the most part, is the do-er; woman is the dreamer. When you write your scene, keep these distinctions in mind. Now and then we might stumble across a nymphomaniac, but most of those are in fiction—and fictional nymphomaniacs don't need sex to establish what they are. What we're reviewing here is the average male and feamale character.

As a male author you must bend over backwards not to make the sex scene a mechanical romp. As a female author you must bend over backwards not to make the sex scene so chimerical the reader wonders if. But fair warning: sooner or later your characters will have to say something to each other. *What* they say reflects their attitudes during the more active confrontation, and this, right here, is where most sex scenes fall apart. Men writers make the characters talk as men do; women writers make the characters talk as women do.

Protect yourself against the misadventure. First, read Robert Browning's poetry and discover hard-as-nails, no-nonsense male logic. Then, read his wife's poetry and be lifted up to a female cloud nine. While he mutters practical things about this being his last duchess, she mutters about loving as far as her soul can reach. Male attitude vs. female attitude. Oversimplified, of course. Whenever I face a paragraph of sex that cannot be avoided, I think of these two people. Chances are, my male character ends up as mundane as a door hinge while the lady flickers like a candle.

Another helpful thought, I suppose, is the idea that each sexual coupling is a "love battle". Borrow your teenager's copy of *Kama Sutra* and that's the first thing you'll learn. Sex activity, some say, is another form of war. Simply put, the male subdues his arch-enemy, the female. Now and then, to break the monotony, things are the other way around. Love bites, some say, tell the tale. So if you follow this premise, let there be war. Have the best sex scene ever. Be the first on your block to get rabies. Make the act of love between your characters sweet and violent. I presume the moment of calm that follows these battles is the same as the moment of calm that comes in a shooting war. Time for peace. Time for reflection. Let's accept this battle premise in our fictional love scenes. Our acceptance might make for character development. Let's make every act of love a telling performance that gives the reader additional insight into our characters. Otherwise, let's edit.

The Power Of Suggestion

I can see you now, staring at me oddly. "What a bore you are," you say. "Novels must tell *everything*."

Oh, I suppose so. Some writers feel that they have to describe every act and sensation of their characters. If that is your kick, go ahead. But fair warning. You will end up with a dirty manuscript—big, fat, crude, and nauseating—that will, for the most part, say absolutely nothing. You will have been so busy counting pores that you will have had no time to get your plot moving. James Joyce might have written a stem-winder of a book, but most of us are not James Joyce. Sex scenes described in clinical detail can, at best, only shock. Also, you *might* have written only smut. Hacks write smut. Let's you and I improve the breed if we can. You *can* write novels without sex scenes. On the other hand, a string of sex alone has yet to make a novel.

Some novels *do* tell all. Sadism, says one, can be fun. Anyone, says another, for sodomy? This one says we must cheer lesbians. Some novels feed off perversions and will continue to feed off them. I'll admit that. But the trouble is, most perverts I know exist only in novels. How many people do you know who practice sodomy? How many teenage nymphets live in your neighborhood? Think hard. Chances are, you've met them for the most part between the covers of a book. In my world, ordinary as it is, people are more concerned with why Johnny can't read, so be careful. I think you live in the same kind of world—and fiction must be based on reality. We can't make up reality any more than we can make up a nymphomaniac.

One final thought and then let's go wash our mouths with soap: the description of people in their birthday suits. It is not that I disapprove of naked women (I am human), but once they're stripped, they're alike in equipment. The difference is their measurements, but if you've described your lady fair elsewhere in your novel—and certainly you should have—we already know if she is or isn't hippy, or bosomy, if she's fat or thin, dumpy or desirable, and the rest. So why belabor her equipment? She's a standard model. Get on with the main event. And to describe a man without his skivvies is a wasted exercise. Why play doctor? How many Raquel Welchs or Warren Beattys live on your street? After all, ordinary people get involved, don't they? Otherwise, where do urchins come from? Greek gods and goddesses are swell, but face facts. Your reader is more familiar with the crowd at PTA.

And, really, wasn't that what *Peyton Place* was all about?

Chapter 9

Everyone Laughed When
I Sat Down at the Typewriter

Should you (ha ha) put humor in your novel?

By all means, but edit out the *ha ha's*. A nut who enjoys his own humor is worse than television's canned laughter. Parenthesized *ha ha's* anesthetize readers. The parenthesized *ha ha* is as distasteful as Peter Pan shouting, "Oh, the cleverness of *me!*" Jokes should make others laugh, not convulse the teller. An occasional smile by the jokester is, I suppose, all right, but you know what I'm driving at. *Ha ha's* are not the magic that makes a sentence funny. If *ha ha's* are your idea of humor, don't write funny novels. Wear lampshades.

There is no magic dust we can sprinkle on words to make them belly laughs.

But don't think you lack a sense of humor. We all have senses of humor. The everyday we endure is filled with funny things, though not all of them are knee-slappers. Your sense of humor might not be the greatest—some senses of humor are whimsical, some are wild, and some are sick—but no one goes from birth to death as deadpanned as Buster Keaton does. Morticians laugh. So do hangmen. And so do the men they hang. Thus, since you *do* possess a sense of humor, let your characters, if they are to be well-rounded, possess a sense of humor, too.

Just don't ask for a definition of humor and don't try to define humor yourself. If you dismantle humor as you would an alarm clock, to see what makes it tick, you'll find that both have stopped ticking. Some brave and dreary souls say Thurber was funny because of Method A, Perelman is funny because of Method B, and Marquis was funny because of Method C. These analysts can also prove that aerodynamically the bumble bee can't fly. But to define the undefinable is meat and drink to their souls. Let them, not us, dismantle humor. Humor has many—and no—component parts. Humor is as impossible to define as happiness, the common cold, and a woman's mind. Define humor and poof! humor flies out the window. Besides, what strikes me funny might strike you as dumb. To see a man slip on a banana offers one viewpoint. To be the one who slips offers another. Beauty is in the eye of the beholder, so is humor, and for that matter, so is ugliness. We don't all cry at the same things. Why, then, should we all laugh?

To be a riot at parties is not to be a riot as a novelist. At parties others may laugh (politely?) but this doesn't make you a (Milton Berle.) When they do laugh, do they laugh early in the evening or later when everything seems hilarious? If the latter is the case, they would also laugh if you fell out of a window, eight floors up. To get laughs from people who are three sheets to the wind is one thing. To get laughs from a reader who is stone sober is another. The reader may not know how funny you look in lampshades. All he sees is print.

Natural or Not At All

Natural humor is better than forced humor. You're writing a novel, not a joke book. Let the humor, if it comes, come naturally. Don't push humor into places humor doesn't fit, but don't avoid humor when it appears. The setting might possess humor. Fine. The reaction of a character might possess humor. Fine. But don't read a joke book, pick out the dandies, and put them in your novel. Suppose the reader read the joke book, too, and what was funny to you was a drag to him? Better to let your own humor bubble. Everyday life has humor. Write it, but don't belabor it or say *ha ha*. Throw the joke book away. Real life is silly enough.

Provided your humor isn't forced and happens *naturally*, several ways exist for you to put humor in your novel. One way could be the setting. Bear in mind that illogical settings (our His and Her space ships) are not as funny, or as believable, as logical settings. The shopping center, for instance, could be a place of high comedy. Suppose Hilda and Herbert went there every night at nine-thirty to kiss in the dark. What do they do during the Christmas buying spree when the center stays open to midnight and there are no dark corners to kiss in? Should they, perhaps, kiss in the parking lot while urchins shout "Merry Christmas" at them? Should they, perhaps, hurry to the music shop, go into a listening booth, and smooch in time to "Jingle Bells"?

> "Herbert you're the man. Think of some place. My feet are cold."
> "Cold feet, warm heart," Herbert said.
> "Get lost," said Hilda.

Had they always kissed in a dark alley, this conversation would never have happened. The reader is as sad as Hilda is because he knows she likes to kiss. But the reader is, one hopes, a little amused by the pickle his friends are in. Having written the above, the idea of finding humor in that scene strikes me as dull, but that's life. I'll leave the idea in as another proof of an earlier point: analyse humor and poof! there it goes again.

Let's take another tack. Humor can be injected into your novel by the wild use of ordinary words. Was it Perelman or was it Leacock who wrote that classic line:

> "Shut up," explained the policeman.

No matter. If such heady stuff comes easily to you, three cheers. Tinker with words but don't overdo the tinkering. Better to have a single gem in every chapter than a dozen in every paragraph.

Humor is everywhere. So unless you're writing a novel about somewhere else, your novel will contain at least a few flashes of wit. Certainly you've read operating room scenes: serious business that, wouldn't you say? But operating rooms contain more cutting up than the surgeon himself does. Quick humor lessens tensions. Or is it that humor exists because tension exists? Humor in an operating room does not reduce the medical profession to levity, of course, because the event is a serious one. But because in real life we find doctors untwanging their twanging nerves with humor, we find humor also in novels. Or. consider battlefields you've seen in movies, read about in novels, or attended personally when bullets were flying. Now we all agree that someone shooting bullets at us is serious business. But now and then, to relieve the tension or perhaps because of near-hysteria, someone cracks a joke. Then, *zip*! here comes another bullet! The joke doesn't stop the flight of the bullet, but the joke does put the bullet in its rightful place in the scheme of things. Without humor, battlefields would be hardly worth the visit. Humor allows the soldier—and the doctor—to keep their part of the human race in true perspective. Same applies to lost souls waiting in death row. When offered a cigarette, one answered:

"No, I think I'll cut down."

The reverse is true and important to remember. Just as operating rooms and battlefields need humor, humorous incidents and characters need moments of solemnity. Charlie Chaplin was hilarious, but now and then he made you cry. For a character to be a non-stop laugh riot from Page One to The End is for that character not to be real. No one —in his right mind, that is—will be cracking jokes *all* the time. Clowns have serious moments and undertakers giggle. The point is, if you write a *humorous* novel or if your novel contains a humorous character don't go overboard. Give your novel serious moments. Give the character serious moments. Read P.G. Wodehouse and see what I mean. Funny characters? Yes and no. His writing is light, but Wodehouse creates well-rounded characters. When the sky is falling down, they don't act silly or make jokes. Like us, they stand around and worry. Every play, book, or movie these days justifies the villain's meanness. The same should be true of comic characters. The buffoon may behave like an idiot, but he does it to grab a handful of stars. Only when he behaves that way and *doesn't* reach for stars will his idiocy be painful—and unreal.

What's So Funny About That?

Not everything is funny to everybody—and especially at the *same* time. So do yourself a favor. If you do use comedy in your novel, let it be humor *most* everybody can understand. No inside jokes, please, or jokes that are so regional the reader, who lives two states away, doesn't know why everyone is laughing. You've been to class reunions, haven't you, where idiots stand around, *remembering*?

"What about when Sue and Frank went on the hayride and. . ."

Wild laughter.

"And what about the basketball game when Lou. . ."

Wild laughter.

Or is there silence? What I mean is, *what* about them? Those who attended the school needn't finish the story. They *know* what happened when Sue and Frank were on the hayride, and Lou was at that basketball game. They know but we don't. If you're an outsider attending your spouse's class reunion you wonder why anyone laughs at all? There are no punch lines and hardly any stories. What is funny to them draws a blank with you. You have no alternative but to smile weakly. If in your humor the reader fails to find what is funny, he too may smile weakly and close the book.

Humor has no set pattern. Thurber approached subject A differently than Wodehouse did. Perelman is not a Benchley and doesn't try to be. On the other hand, Benchley is no Leacock. Each treats the subject from his own point of view. Some people think Dick Van Dyke is the greatest. Some prefer Lucille Ball. This group likes Henny Youngman, that group likes Jack Paar, and in the corner another group—for some reason—think Lyndon B. Johnson is a riot. Live and let live. To each his own. You have humor in you—your own brand—and it's yours. No one will ever have a sense of humor quite like yours again. To one man a pie in the face is hilarious, but to another it's a sloppy way to eat. So don't try to copy this humorist's style. Or that humorist's. You can't. Let the humor in you bubble to the surface. It may be slapstick or whimsy, but it's yours.

Here's a sad thought. When you use humor in your novel, use it with the knowledge that not everyone will enjoy it. Expect this to happen because it will. Look at the brighter side: if the same things struck all of us funny, the world would be dull, wouldn't it? Anyway, what makes you think your sense of humor is so stunning that it will hit everyone where he lives? Even the great humorists lack this power. If your sense of humor is that brilliant, don't waste time writing novels. Go to Hollywood. Head to Broadway. Show business has been waiting since Hector was a pup for the writer whose stuff was funny one hundred percent of the time. But if you're like the rest of us, suffering the disadvantages of being human, you'll get smart and not even try to please all of the people all of the time. Humans must deal with humans who are human, too. You can't make jokes with a computer. Canned laughter is one thing. Human laughter is another. To prove that no one is perfect, I modestly offer Exhibit A: myself. After I had outlined this book, I passed the outline along to the publisher who passed the outline along to other professional writers to see if this book answered the need. One writer—a charming fellow—commented on my use of humor. "Keep it in the book," he said. Another writer—a nasty man who hates Christmas—commented also on my use of humor. "A bit forced, wouldn't you say?" he said. Did I cry? Well, not in public anyway. But I should have known what I'm now passing along to you: you can't please them all, so why try' Please yourself. Period.

Now if you will excuse me, I'm going to try on lampshades.

Chapter 10

Having Something to Say—and Letting Your Characters Say it

Our personalities, like our fingerprints, are uniquely our own. Hide your personality—the real you that's deep inside—as you will, nonetheless your novel will bear your personality's imprint. Even should you write with the detachment of a cold fish, *who* you are and *what* you are will shine from every page. For example, the moment you choose to do the love scene this way instead of that way shows these things. Frightening thought, isn't it? When you write a novel you expose yourself to strangers.

Well, novels always do. That's the way writing is. Can you keep yourself out of your novel? Never. Face the fact that the minute your novel goes on sale, friends and strangers will know you—intimately. Be reticent if you like. Your novel can reveal things even your psychiatrist won't know. But the question at this point is, how much should you as the author *intentionally* intrude? If your novel is a first-person exercise, some of this question is answered. When Uncle Fuddles tells the tale from his point of view there is little room left for yours. But if your novel is *not* a first-person effort—you as the writer *tell* what happens to the characters—should you toss in your own feelings about the characters, their attitudes, their morality, and the way they slurp their coffee? Should you, perhaps, enter the novel with a paragraph like this:

> Hilda hated Herbert. She had the right. Girls don't like gents what get fresh at covered-dish dinners. I know because once in Oberlin, Ohio, I met a fellow who. . .

And on and on.

Far-fetched? No author in his right mind would stop the action of his novel to interject views like that? Perhaps not. If he does, chances are the novel will not be published. That technique went out with Thackeray. Authors these days do not lecture. This makes sense. If a reader wants a lecture, he will attend one advertised as such. But since novels are advertised as novels, authors should stay clear of "That reminds me of the time in Florence, Kentucky, when this fat lady wearing a funny hat said to me. . ."

As suggested, when your novel is first-person, perhaps from Hilda's point of view, you have no room to play. All points of view will be hers. Unless in real life you *are* Hilda, lectures—with or without colored slides—are deadly. And even if you are Hilda in real life, cool it.

On the other hand, don't hesitate to speak out—from your heart. Make sure though that what you say adds and doesn't detract. If your reader believes in your characters, he might just believe in you, too, which would be nice, don't you think? This means he might buy whatever point you're selling. So why sell him something cheap? Sell him what you, yourself, believe with all your might. What you sell (the "message" of your novel) need not be lofty. The points some novels make are simple things, but they are honest and have value. Perhaps you feel the world is grubby morally. Show this moral grubbiness by means of your characters. But whenever you have something of value to say, better let your characters say it. Don't mount a podium. To deliver *that* kind of message, send a telegram.

Are you shy? Well, Emily Dickinson, shyness will get you nowhere—and history proved that, didn't it, honey? Your poetry knew joy but you didn't. Forget your inhibitions. Don't try to hide that warm you behind a cold style. The reader will still see you. If he's going to see you anyway, better let him see the real you. But throw yourself obliquely into your novel. Be obvious and you'll make an ass of yourself. A Jesuit once said, "The straight line is the shortest distance between two points." And, he added, "But they can always see you coming." Remember that when you make this or that point in your novel. Readers don't read novels to be lectured. When you make your Great Point, make sure the reader doesn't see you coming.

Do Your Characters Show How You Feel?

The real question of this chapter is, should an author intrude in any fashion in his plot or should he let his characters stumble about, finding grief or joy on their own, without his indirect value judgments? Some writers prefer to make no judgments. Perhaps you are of that school too. I'm not. Thus, I must write my novels *my* way, am fond of my characters, and fond of my readers. To go this route of laying your heart on the line, though, you must be prepared for the reader who disagrees with your values or, worse, the reader who makes fun of you.

Look at the question this way. Fictional characters can be anything we are capable of creating, but the same does not hold true for us. Real people can not be something they are not. To me this business of adopting a detached pose is phony. To you it may not be. I suggest that we can make our characters into whatever we wish, but we can't change ourselves. We are what we are. If you, in real life, are warm and friendly, be that way as a writer, too. Lay your heart on the line with every word you write. Don't try to be the fellow your mother thinks you are. When you write, my friend, be yourself. Write honestly. If you don't lay your heart on the line, giving strangers the tools with which to destroy you, you will have written phony trash. If you're not going to say what's in your soul, why write a book at all? So write—and let the critics sneer. You will have done the best you could. You'll have at least that satisfaction.

Which person—in real life—would you rather meet? The cheerful hypocrite or the plain old guy who mumbles? The hypocrite plays life cool, says only what people want to hear, and when he's alone, he's not certain who he really is. The plain old guy lets you know exactly where he stands, even if you don't approve of where he stands. The hypocrite says everything is nice or bad, depending on what his audience wishes to hear. The plain old guy is not afraid to mumble how nice things are nice. If you'd rather read a wishy-washy book, you're not my kind of people. And, for the matter, you're not many people's kind of people. Even hypocrites distrust hypocrites. Don't write what you feel the editor or the readers want to read. Write what you *must*.

You Can't Win 'Em All

Just as with humor, when you write from the heart you will not please everyone. So don't expect to. Television networks try to please us all, end up pleasing none, and thus change shows so often every night is amateur night. You don't please everyone in real life, do you? Why expect to do so in your novel? Your novel, after all, is only an extension of yourself. No matter which side of an argument you choose, some- where someone will choose the other side. But if you don't take sides at all, you're a gutless wonder. And even being that you can't win. Other gutless wonders will step on you. So this business—and life—is damned if you do and damned if you don't. Might as well, with every novel you write, lay your heart on the line, do the best you can, and go for broke.

"Ah," you say, "if I wrote what I really thought, I'd be run out of town. You see, sir, my neighbors consider me nice."

Well, write what you think, then grab the first bus.

Writing is an extension of yourself. Writing puts the real you on dis- play, not the "you" you offer to the PTA. Bare your soul and take your chances. Have a ball. If you are a free spirit, be a free spirit in print. If you're a mean bastard, be a mean bastard. Don't try to hide behind the face you show your friends. What you say in print—and how you say it —will strip your mask away. Anyway, if writing what you think loses you a friend, good riddance. He wouldn't have liked the real you to begin with.

Keep nothing in reserve. When you write your novel toss in every- thing but the kitchen sink. Don't save this thought or that character for your next novel. If you don't write this one right, there'll be no next time. Forget your friends. Forget the critics. To write a novel is to commune with a typewriter. Don't hold back. If what you are is good, this goodness will show. Don't be afraid to be considered corny. No matter how sophisticated we presume we are, a guy in the next block is always more so. Don't write bland fluff that they will label "a charming little volume. . ."

Apply logic. If all your friends und every critic bought your novel, you'd still not peddle enough copies to realize more than your advance. Why write to please anyone but yourself? If what you write is corny, so be it. If what you write is stuffy, so be that, too. But does what you write please you? That is the question.

Now and then, to keep your reader hanging in, use the trick used in advertising, especially if your novel is a first-person novel with one viewpoint only. Include the reader. A premise in advertising is: "Get the reader involved in the product." Your product is your novel. In advertising, copywriters get the reader involved by talking at him point-blank.

> "You'll like our new sewer systems. . ."
> "Have you tried our LSD lately?"
> "When are you going to. . ."
> "Have you heard about. . ."
> "Here's a new product for you. . ."

You, you, you, you!

For instance, in one of my novels, a character discusses girls and pinball machines:

> You can take pinball machines or leave them alone. After a game they don't come around—their lights blinking and their flippers flipping—to ask you to say nice things to them. That's the difference between pinball machines and girls. Pinball machines don't make demands on you, don't get angry when you tilt them, and they got more free games than that guy has pills. There are no free games with girls. You spend a nickle on them and they don't even light up.

In a third-person novel where the author himself tells what happens, the "you" device doesn't work too well. A paragraph like the one above would not fit a third-person novel. The author himself then would be telling the reader:

> You can take pinball machines or leave them alone. . .

The reader would stop, wonder who was talking to him,—there's the author caught flat-footed in the middle of a paragraph where he had no right to be—and the plot stops. In such situations, revise.

> Doolie could take pinball machines or leave them alone. After a game they didn't come around—their lights blinking and their flippers flipping—to ask him to say nice things to them. . .

Same thought, you see, but the plot moves swiftly along. Ain't that nice? The reader doesn't buy novels to have authors lecture him on the merits of a pinball machine, does he? But he will sit still if one of your characters lectures. Whatever message you're peddling should never come from you, but from one of your characters. Why be vain? If the point you want to make is a good one, what do you care who makes it? To make the point is the important thing. That's why you wrote your novel.

The point of *this* chapter, as you must have grasped by now, is that novels worth their salt do make points and have messages. Another point of this chapter is that the message to have worth must come from your heart. Accept that somewhere, someone upon reading your novel will be shocked, bewildered, or bored. But be yourself. Right now, before doing another thing with your novel, think of all the things you'd like to put in your book if only Uncle Fuddles wouldn't read it. Then, put them in. Write the novel you *must* write. A phony one will never be published. Understand that here and now. If you are a loudmouth who inside is tender, what do you care what the other loudmouths think? Write a tender novel. Other people—somewhere—are tender, too. They'll understand. Write the novel you must write. Just don't try to be something you're not. You might get away with it in real life. In print, you don't stand a chance.

Better be yourself.

Chapter 11

The Way It Was—Exactly

Whether your first novel is about the blonde down the street or your grandpappy as a child, you will write a historical novel. Stay calm. Don't panic. Some people write historical novels by design. The rest of us write them by default.

The *formal* historical novel, a novel that's advertised as such, shows life in the Sixteenth Century, tells about the Pilgrims, or trafficks with Abraham Lincoln. These novels take mounds of research. One is not supposed to make up history. And one can not remember back that far. To research our novels, located in present time, is easier. Ah, we say, all we have to do is remember what happened last month, or the month before that. What makes you think we're writing a *historical* novel? Come off it.

Can't—and here's why. I'll agree that the novel you write will have to do with *today* or will start *last year* and bring us up to today where your happy ending is. But to write your novel will take at least six months. Even if a publisher accepted your manuscript the next day, to manufacture and market your novel will take another nine months. Thus before a reader can read about the *today* of your novel, fifteen months will have elapsed. The *today* you meant will mean nearly a year and a half ago for the reader. We fix a moment in time, put characters in that moment, let them kiss a lot, but whatever moment we fix in time, to the reader that moment is history. We have, by default, written a historical novel. So with that as the known, let's at least make our settings and characters accurate so we can say:

"There! Last year or last century, this is the way things really were."

In an earlier chapter we glanced at research that had to do with settings. Now let's take a good, hard look at the subject to become *expert* researchers. After all, even in fiction there are facts. Keep your facts straight. Don't have your grandmother, a young hellion in the Gay Nineties, appear as an ingenue on a Major Bowes' circuit. Don't have an urchin born about the time of Pearl Harbor remember the Maine. Don't allow your characters to ride in autos that were not invented. And remember, the Pilgrims never heard of Culligan's Soft Water; Avon wasn't calling, God was. If in your novel your characters get stuck in ten-foot snow drifts in Buffalo, get the day of the big snow right. Let it snow the wrong day and a reader will sound off:

"Couldn't have snowed that Tuesday. I remember because on that Tuesday I had my teeth pulled and the sun was shining."

Don't question his gumming. He will be right and you will be wrong. People remember dates for the darnedest reasons. Never underestimate a reader's memory, be his teeth real or storebought. If he doesn't recall the date because of the misadventure with the dentist, he will remember it because that was the day his three-horse parlay paid off, his wife ran off with the butcher, and he got arrested for arson at sea. He'll never forget that day as long as he lives. Check the weather bureau. Make it snow in your novel when it snowed in Buffalo. Your characters are imaginary. To shovel snow is not.

How To Make Sure

Research means checking facts. Simple as that. The best way to check facts is to go to the library or local newspaper office. Research *can* be fun. Leafing through stacks of dusty old newspapers—and I assure you, they are dirty; don't try to keep your hands clean—can open more doors for your imagination than all the remembering in the world. Besides, to check back issues is quicker and more efficient. Why *wonder* when you can check the files and *know?*

Suppose a character in your novel was a teenager right after World War One. Head to the newspaper office—or library—and ask to see the bound issues of newspapers for 1918. Tell the people why you want to look and they'll be pleased to oblige. What you'll get will be a huge and musty volume that might contain anywhere from three months of that newspaper to the full year. The size of the volume depends on the number of pages each long-ago edition contained. Because a newspaper or library usually has only one such volume available, chances are they will not allow you to lug the book home. You wouldn't want to. Writers have problems enough without inviting back strain. But you will be allowed to find a quiet corner at the newspaper or library and look through the ancient newspapers as long as you like. You will be reminded not to tear out any interesting items, which makes sense, doesn't it? This book they give you is the only copy. You or someone else might want to look through those pages again years from now. If some dullard has stolen a page or so, that's all, Charlie. You can't read what isn't there. So bring along notebook and pencils. That's the ticket.

Only there you sit. Now, what on earth should you look for? Your characters are imaginary. Certainly you'll not find stories about *them* in the old newspaper. But you can find out a lot about the times your characters "lived." First, read a few editions from cover to cover: news, ads, comics, sports, financial, society, everything! Make any notes you like. You will have, by then, dipped into the time—and place—your characters lived when they were young. Your hands will be dirty but your heart will soar. At last you will be able to add touches of this and touches of that, so an old-timer, upon reading your book, will say:

"Yep. That's exactly the way things were. Why, I'd forgotten how . . ."

Develop your own research method. I have mine. Don't accept my way as gospel. What I do is read the grocery ads, noting prices. Today's reader is slackjawed with wonder at the low price those days of a good steak. To see if vaudeville was in its heyday—or to find what was—I read the amusement pages. Now and then I strike gold. A star today was, back then, a second banana in vaudeville's five-a-day. I slip this fact in my novel. *Real* history, you might say. I check automobile prices, the makes of cars, and how they are equipped. Some of the cars —and the equipment—prove hilarious. I check sports pages to find who the heroes were. To see how cheap homes were, I check real estate listings—and wish I were dead. I see how much houses and flats rented for. Where has the dollar fled! A reading of the help-wanted ads shows me jobs that no longer are offered these days. Sad. But all is grist for our mill. Read on. Look at the pictures of the ladies. Ignore the high-fashion stuff from Paris. Concentrate on what the lady wears at her party to raise funds for drunken sailors. That way you'll know precisely how the ladies dressed. Three cheers for button-shoes, and look, is she wearing a bustle? Check styles that men wear, too. They're not a put-on, they're for real. By the time you've leafed through three months of old newspapers, your eyes will begin to blur, but you will have, in addition to a splitting headache, a fistful of notes and new ideas of how things back then were—*exactly*.

Newspapers Have Changed Too

If you wish to research a particular event (a flood, a murder, or the sky falling down) you might want to copy the story word for word from the paper and take it home. Fine, but use caution. The more ancient the newspaper, the more flowery the reporter. Some ancient reporters, I am both sorry and pleased to suggest, wrote as much fiction in their news stories as they wrote fact. Better sift for the bare bones of the event you seek. Avoid the embellishments. Ignore the icing. Was the crowd that big? Did the lady really scream a sentence that long? You might wish to include the story as it stands in your novel. Can you? Well, ask the current editor. Chances are, he'll grant permission. Seek written permission. You don't need a battery of lawyers at your side. Nothing fancy. A simple note from the editor to you will suffice. Intent is what you wish to show—that your intentions are honest and so are the intentions of the editor. I know, I know. Your brother is a lawyer and wants to draw up a fancy document. "Short notes," he warns, "can be tossed out of court." Sure, but so can long contracts. Don't make your life more complicated than it is. Get simple releases. Offer an editor a complicated release that runs on forever and chances are, he'll not sign. I know I wouldn't. A hidden clause might give you the right to kick my dog. Just remember this: when you run that piece in your novel, you will credit the source. No footnotes, please. Keep it simple.

Have one of your characters read the story from that edition. Name the edition. There, send your brother home.

Back issues of the newspaper will give you the local scene. What about the national scene and the world back then? Read back issues of *Time* Magazine. Newspapers, being closer to the source, are better on local events, but *Time*, being national, looks at the larger canvas. Read back issues of *Time*—or *Newsweek* because I'm not peddling either, they're both peachy—to fit your characters into the world that existed beyond the city limits. Newspapers, of course, cover national and international news, but by their nature, they cover this news on a daily basis. Many times the background is not there. Newspapers presume their readers are aware of the background. *Time*, on the other hand, writes each event as a news essay which gives you more background than you'll need in a month of Sundays. Thus, national and international research don't take long. And, happily, a day spent at it will save you errors later. You will put the Spanish War in the years it was and you'll know where Pearl Harbor belongs, too. *Time* makes sure you have the right President in the White House, though you can't be far wrong to use the name Roosevelt. To research that period before *Time* began publishing, seek the other national magazines of the earlier days, for instance, *Literary Digest*. Be leery of its opinion polls, though. Try popular magazines like the *Saturday Evening Post* which ran articles as well as Horatio Hornblower and Tugboat Annie. But be smart. Check not only the editorial content, check the ads, too, and see what milady hankered for. To research periods even before those heady days means you are definitely writing a *formal* historical novel. Well, those things aren't my meat. I can't help you, and I won't, because any ideas I'd have for researching those babies would be hearsay. I'd only be talking through my hat. The title of this book is not *How To Write Any Kind Of Book That Strikes Your Fancy*. The title of this book is *One Way To Write Your Novel*.

Quotable Quotes

What about quoting people—instead of newspapers—from the past? Just make certain the personages are either dead or that their quotes have appeared in so many newspapers or magazines that what they said is public domain and not copyrighted. To quote Governor Hothead's public utterances that were reported, verbatim, in a newspaper is one thing. To quote him from a personal letter he wrote to a chorus girl—a letter that was never released publicly—is another. That letter is personal property. A quote from a book he himself wrote—or someone wrote about him—might be a violation of copyright. When in doubt, don't quote. Your book is not about the governor anyway—at least, not *that* much about him. But above all, when you quote, quote accurately. Quote accurately. I can't stress this point enough. Quote accurately. Make sure the quote—if only a sentence lifted from a ten-hour fillibuster—says exactly what the speaker *intended* to say. Quoting out of context is dirty pool. You've seen that sort of hanky panky. A movie critic writes:

> This movie is perfectly awful. It could have been glorious, but somebody goofed. Don't see it. You'll not miss it.

Yet, the movie advertising features his quote:

> Perfectly. . .glorious. Don't. . .miss it.

Same is true with lifting one sentence, complete, from a paragraph.

> Governor Hothead said today, "Sure, I'll run for governor again. I'll run when hell freezes over, and not before!"

When you quote correctly old Hothead saying, "Sure, I'll run for governor again." is that what he really said? Lifting a sentence out of context can change that sentence's meaning. Sometimes, to aid our plot, we find ourselves wishing the governor had said one thing and not the other. But to quote a real person out of context makes him not a real person, but a character we have created and manipulated. That's why I say, quote where and when you can, but make certain your quotes use not only his words but his meaning, too. Otherwise don't quote—and you can quote me on that!

While back issues of newspapers give your characters the feel of the town and back issues of *Time*—or *Newsweek*—give your characters the feel of the world beyond the town, I suggest two other volumes that can help you:

> 1. Any worthwhile almanac (I prefer *Reader's Digest Almanac and Yearbook,* published by Funk & Wagnall)
> 2. *An Encyclopedia of World History* (Houghton-Mifflin)

Suppose one of your characters plays the horses. One of mine did. I know nothing about horses but whoa and giddap. But thanks to the *Reader's Digest Almanac* I could put more wise words into the mouth of my character than I could into my own. I had him recite the winners of the Kentucky Derby, Preakness Stakes, and Belmont Stakes, name the jockeys, and talk about the dollars involved. I had him know which hayburners won the Triple Crown, which the *Reader's Digest Almanac* informed me happened only when some horse won in the same year the Derby, Preakness, and Belmont. The *Reader's Digest Almanac's* memory is better than any race tout's. My character sounded real and so will yours.

The *Encyclopedia of World History* is a book I can—and can't—get excited about. When I don't need it, the book is a drag. When I do need it, the book is worth its weight in gold. The *Reader's Digest Almanac* fills me in on the current odds and ends of life, but the *Encyclopedia of History* fills me in on everything else—and then some. If I have a character who comes of age before *Time* saw the light of day, I turn to the history encyclopedia. It will tell me everything—and more—than I care to know about 1903. This encyclopedia, like the thesaurus, takes getting used to in order to know where to look for things in it. But the time you spend learning how to use the *Encyclopedia of World History* will be worth every minute you invested.

Although as I type this I feel that you should go out and *buy* every book I mention (including the ones *I* write), I will suggest that most of these books are, or should be, available at the library. So spend a few evening there and get to know the librarians, who are sharp cookies. They can help you in more ways than one, but I'll let them suggest the ways.

The point of this chapter is uncomplicated. This is how I do research.

Instant research, it could be called. I simply don't trust that old lady down the street to remember how 1912 really was. People do not have total recall and I don't expect them to have it. But books do. Old newspapers do. Back issues of magazines do. The novel you're going to write probably won't need much research effort, but what must be researched must be researched. Let that be our school song. Then when you create that long-ago yesterday—last week or last decade—you can truthfully tell your characters:

"Have fun, kids. This is exactly the way things were. *Exactly.*"

Chapter 12

Plotting: First, Last, and Middle Chapters

Sooner or later your novel must be plotted. *Plotted*? What's that? Plotting is the making of the blueprint, the design which tells you where the bricks and boards (scenes and description) go. To build a house without a blueprint just isn't done. The blueprint might only exist in the builder's mind. Most likely, though, somewhere he's scribbled some rough notes. He doesn't want his completed house to look like something the cat dragged in. You don't want your completed novel to *read* that way, either. Plotting means to outline, in whatever fashion you like, the plot you will fill out with words and paragraphs and chapters. Before we plot your first novel—and we will—let's look at plotting in general, which is an easier way of getting our feet wet. After all, why make writing a novel more complicated than it is? Three cheers for the easy way out!

Let's start like this. When you tell a joke—unless you're my wife— you will save the punch line for last. The same is true of a murder mystery. We'll not tell the reader in the first chapter that the butler did it. If our story is about lovers and we know, from the beginning she will say yes, those nine chapters of her saying no are a drag. If Herbert is going to climb Mount Everest and our novel is of his adventure getting up there, we certainly won't begin chapter one with him sitting on top, wiggling his toes, and eating a ham sandwich. Readers like a little suspense in their novels, so give it to them. Keep them in doubt till the last paragraph if you can. Will the guy get the girl? Will Mount Everest be scaled? Will the ham sandwich taste good? This is what plotting is all about.

"Don't need to plot *my* novel," you say. "That stuff just flows from my typewriter."

Bully for you—I think. But I have the feeling that any writer who lets stuff "flow" from his typewriter sooner or later stops the flow, gathers up the debris, sits in a quiet corner, and says:

"Okay, okay. I got a lot written but what have I got?"

Letting stuff "flow" simply won't do. You will see that *this* character has become stronger than *that* character, which was not our intention at all. You will discover another character taking an attitude you didn't want him to take. Your love scenes will have the wrong people in a chinch. Characters will talk a lot—rave on for pages, in fact—but they rave about subjects that have nothing to do with your story. You might even find the weather whopperjawed. One minute your characters shiver in the snow and the next they pant in the sun because, somewhere in the "flowing," you misplaced spring.

To read an *un*plotted novel— one that does not move logically from beginning to end—is the same as eating a fancy dinner at which none of the courses appear when they should. Dessert comes before the meat course. Soup arrives whenever the waiter thinks about it. After-dinner drinks and cigars come when the rolls and butter do. Where the salad is no one knows and most are afraid to ask. Would you eat a meal like that or do you prefer a semblance of order? Well, who wants to read a novel that has no basic design? I'd rather read a dictionary, and with some of these free-flowing novels, I think I have.

To write a novel without a plan in mind is to waste energy. You'll write scenes you don't need. Your characters will talk at the wrong time. Your book will be like Stephen Leacock's cowboy who jumped on his horse and rode off in all directions. Why be obscure when to plot your novel is not that difficult? A plot can even make you feel better. For instance, as suggested earlier, let's say you're going to write a simple two hundred page novel that has twenty chapters of ten pages each. You can write—or plot—only one chapter at a time. Already you can relax. Already plotting has made your task less complicated. You are not concerned with plotting two hundred pages. Your only concern is plotting ten. When you get those ten plotted, you plot ten more, then ten more, and one fine day you can say:

"Holy Typewriter Ribbon! I've plotted a book!"

So let's move easily into this business of plotting. There's no rush. Your book will have twenty chapters and you know, generally, what your story is about. The first problem is, how to keep the plot interesting to other people until they reach *The End*, or would you rather be precious and write *finis*? Plotting, of course, is the answer to holding the reader's interest. So let's consider your first chapter.

What Must The First Chapter Do?

Before you hold his interest, first you must get it. Let's make rough notes, nothing fancy or formal, and see what happens. Plotting will tell you what the first chapter must do. Well, what *must* it do? Introduce a character or two to the reader? Good thinking. Write that down. Should the first chapter give us a hint whether the character is a good guy or bad buy? Write down your answer; it's your book, not mine. Note also that you must tell the reader what the character looks like. Now, what else for chapter one? Well, if your novel is about the guy chasing the girl, you might just introduce the guy—and his loneliness; or the girl—and hers; or both. Dealer's choice. But somewhere for your first chapter make a note that you must establish, reasonably so, what *kind* of novel you're writing: love story, mystery, heavy literature, or farce. Note with another simple sentence what "happens" in the first chapter. What "happens" could be a lot or a little. The important thing is not to tip your hand and tell, in the first chapter, what will happen in the rest of the book. Keep the reader interested—but guessing. Now, set aside the rough notes for chapter one. Those notes, by the way, can be called plotting, blocking, or chicken scratches, whichever you prefer.

Take another blank sheet of paper and do the same thing with the *last* chapter in your book. Note in this chapter what has been resolved. And, stop looking at me like that, saying, "How can I plot the last chapter until I've plotted all the other chapters that come before it?" Easy as pie, really. You are writing a novel. A novel follows a logical course from beginning to end. Before you start you should, as the author, know what the end will be. If you don't know, you're kidding yourself. You'll not be writing a novel. You'll only be improving your typing speed. Plot your last chapter, sketch it out with a few brief sentences, and let your last chapter serve as the True North for your novel. Later on, when you start writing, you'll know instantly when any character or paragraph will not help you reach True North. To type words that don't carry you straight to the conclusion of your novel is to waste your time—and the reader's. No side excursions to see the rainbow, please. Stay on course. Why write aimlessly? Aim for True North, your last chapter.

So there you are. You've plotted the first and final chapter. You know pretty much now what they must contain. Now all that remains is —ugh!—to plot the chapters in between which, believe me, is easier done than explained. Oversimplified, you'll have something like this in front of you:

Chapter 1: Herbert meets Hilda.
Chapter 20: They marry.

Look upon your novel as a movie you're seeing. Mind you, I'm not suggesting you write a book in the hope that Hollywood will make a movie of it; Hollywood will make hash of it. But I'm saying let's pretend that instead of writing a book you are watching a movie. A movie is made up of many scenes and many happenings, all of which carry the audience from start to finish. One scene will no more make a feature-length motion picture than one incident will make a novel. So come back to your plotting, put away the buttered popcorn, and look upon each chapter as a separate movie scene. Let one chapter throw an obstacle into the patch of Herbert and Hilda. Perhaps, as her boss, he must fire her. Let another chapter show her fighting back: she hides his key to the men's room. On and on you go, heading to True North, your final chapter. As you plot, you will occasionally think up scenes that you have no room for. Hang on to them. Later you might decide to kill one old scene and insert the new one. Nothing in your novel, at this stage, should be considered final except the True North that is the pay-off of your plot. Whatever your characters do in the chapter, they must do to reach True North. Writing in a logical manner is an art; plotting helps us master that art.

Also, as a bonus, plotting helps you this way: when you at last sit at the typewriter, your plot outline in front of you, and begin to write this or that chapter, you'll not hesitate. You will know exactly what you must make that chapter do. Plotting has another advantage as well: when the day comes you're scheduled to write that scene of violence and you don't feel up to it, you can put that scene aside and write one that strikes your fancy more. Skip around. All chapters are going to the same True North. There will be days you feel like laboring over description. Fine. Find a chapter that needs such tinkering and labor. There will be days when the idea of dialogue appeals more. Check your plotting notes. Find a chapter that needs conversation. The days will adjust themselves; everything that needs to be written will be written. You might have to force yourself a day here and there, but with this method you'll use less force than if you had no method at all. Without a definite plan in mind and with no True North to aim for, you might still be floundering with chapter one.

As you chug along, plotting chapter after chapter, you will move through eighteen unknown chapters, make them known, and arrive at the last chapter. You, with your plotting, have gone somewhere. But has the book? Review each chapter. Check its action. Does each chapter move the plot forward? Or does the chapter, as we do at times, dawdle? Think in terms of the basic plot, the total of all the scenes. Plots can move characters from one location to another, and on to another, until the book ends. Plots, also, can move the way the clock ticks. This chapter is morning. The last chapter is night. Or plots can move as calenders do. This chapter is January, that one is May, and the last is December. Plots, at times, move with—or against—gravity, down a flight of stairs into Dante's Inferno or up the side of a mountain to a ham sandwich. Does each chapter make the reader aware that movement exists? These are questions you must ask and answer.

Try This Experiment

Lest you consider this difficult, select a novel you know well. Pretend the novel has not been written and that you are going to write it. But first, you must block or plot it. Book in hand, do so. Write a one sentence—two at the most—summary of each chapter. Write with "plot movement" in mind. You know the last chapter. You know how the story ends. See how each chapter gets us there. Then, look at your notes. A wasted exercise? No, no, no. It will change your attitude. Ain't that nice?

Or try this. You could, as some writers do, divide the novel into three loose parts and look upon your novel as a three-act play. A book that contains twenty chapters would be divided, give or take a chapter here and there, into three units of six or seven chapters, each unit representing an act of a play. The trouble with this approach is, you not only plot a novel but learn such non-essential trivia as what makes a good second act curtain. So be it. Any test you can try against your plot to assure you of the plot's soundness is reasonable. With the theatrical approach, your first unit of chapters represents the first act of the play. By the time you reach chapter seven—or thereabouts—you should have, as the first act of a play does, established your main characters. Your characters in act one will be confronted with an impossible task, the completing of which constitutes your last chapter or your final curtain. No matter how hard they try to win in act one, they can't win for losing. Curtain! The curtain for the second act, or perhaps chapter fourteen, is tricky. Your hero thinks he has the problem licked but a few moments before the end of act two, fate pulls the rug out from under him. If fate doesn't hurl him back to where he started from, fate hurls him back beyond his original starting point. The difference, then, is that the audience (the reader) knows what the situation is and how nice your hero is, which is more than the reader knew when he opened the book. In the third act, happily, everything is resolved, usually after one grand confrontation even grander than the second act curtain. Then the curtain comes down and that's it. There isn't any more.

Naturally no one in his right mind would plot a book exactly the way he would plot a play. The theater is one form of communication; the novel is another. But certain premises *do* hold for both. A play moves from beginning to end and, unless it waits for Godot, travels in a logical manner. Some plays, musicals, dawdle for a song or a chorus line, but that's another matter. In the play, as in your novel, every scene and line of dialogue that doesn't pay its way goes out—fast. That's why your book must be plotted, chapter by chapter, so that it moves with no dawdling from start to finish. Long-haired artists might dispute this, but they dispute so much, I am confused. Maintain momentum, I say. It is not the task of the reader to communicate with you. It is your task to communicate with him. After all, he didn't ask you to write the book.

So much for generalities. Let's plot the rest of your novel.

Chapter 13

Your Plotting Notebook for a Novel

Time to plot!

An architect at first has a vague idea of how the completed building will look. At the start you as a novelist have only the same beautiful daydream. But what better starting point for architect and writer than a beautiful dream? To turn that dream into reality we must stop dreaming, though, and be practical. Design your dream home, Mr. Architect, but don't forget the bathroom. Do as the architect must do: set the dream aside and noodle. Plotting is your form of noodling. Here's how to noodle your book.

First, put into a loose-leaf notebook as many blank pages as your book will have chapters. Then, do the easy part. On the first page write *Chapter One*, on the second page write *Chapter Two*, and so on. When you finish you will have a separate page for each chapter. Now, on the page for the first chapter, write a simple sentence: *The guy meets the girl*, or *We meet the guy*, or whatever is your reason for chapter one.

Now, flip over to your last chapter and write another simple sentence: *The guy marries the girl*, or *The guy solves the mystery*, or *He sits up there eating that ham sandwich*, or whatever the True North of your novel is.

So far, so good. Now, before writing another thing ask yourself how many main characters your novel requires. You may not know all of them at this point, but certainly you'll know most. Suppose you decide your novel must have seven main characters. Well, to introduce all seven in the first chapter will confuse your reader and might confuse you, too. If the reader you confuse is the editor in the publishing house, your writing efforts stop before they start. So avoid confusion where you can.Anyway, no one in his right mind can remember seven characters who have been introduced to him in one chapter. And your main characters deserve better than that. They have value as individuals. Figure on introducing them, one at a time, chapter at a time.

With that in mind, go back to your notebook. Let's say, for the moment, you will introduce a new main character at the rate of one per chapter. With seven characters that will take seven chapters, which will give you a reason, then, for those seven chapters, won't it? Leaf through your notebook, and write which character will be introduced in which chapter. Common sense dictates that Hilda and Herbert be introduced right away. The rest of the cast can be introduced, chapter at a time, as needed. Don't brood too much about when to introduce whom. You can always juggle the introductions later. Right at this point, *when* you introduce any character is not final. Your notebook right now is stamped *Temporary*. After all, this is your novel. What's the fun of plotting it if you can't change your mind?

Organizing Your Ideas

Now, consider for a moment the *time* span of your novel. Will the period of its action cover weeks, days, years, hours—or what? Let's say, for now only, that your novel will cover the period of a little more than a year. You want your last chapter to be in December because you plan to have Hilda and Herbert kiss under the mistletoe. Well, if your final chapter is in December, the one before that will be November, the one before that will be October, and there you back, backtracking month at a time, chapter at a time, to see what month the opening chapter will be. Already, in plotting, some of the decisions have been taken out of your hands and you are free to brood about other items. Your novel might open in June, February, or whatever month your outline indicates. You will find that your main characters meet Uncle Fuddles for the first time in August. Isn't that nice to know?

Had you employed a different time span—the twenty-hour hour period—Uncle Fuddles might have made his entrance at ten in the morning because that's the chapter that calls for him to appear. Whatever your time span, go through your notebook and give each chapter its logical place in the sequence. Now as you review the outline a vague picture of your novel begins to emerge, doesn't it?

Let's not linger here. Think about your dream plot again. What *is* your novel about? Guy meeting girl, guy losing girl, guy looking for girl, and guy finding girl again? Suppose your plot is that. Let's go back to the notebook. Before the guy can find the girl *again*—under that mistletoe on Christmas eve—he has to meet her. Well, we know where he will find her *again*: in the final chapter. But in which chapter should he meet her? Chapter one? Chapter two? Please, pal, no later than chapter three, but you name which. Let's suppose he meets her in chapter two. Okay, write that down on the page marked chapter two. You will see, for example, he meets her in September—or at nine in the morning. Your other notations on that page tell you this. Let's move on. After meeting her, he loses her. Right? Now, does he spend the bulk of your novel trying to find her again, or does he lose her pretty far along in the story? Which does your plot call for? Anyway, on one of the chapter pages write that *this* is where he loses her. You might find he loses her when Uncle Fuddles arrives on the scene. This fact comes from your other, and earlier, notes. Also, you'll then know what time (month, day, or hour) he loses her. Thus your outline supplies you with information you hadn't expected. Plotting outlines this way offers us many wonderful and, at times, surprising surprises. Write in which chapters he looks for her, in which chapters he sometimes gives up hope. List all these things. Keep in mind the first and second act curtains we talked about.

Plant Now, Dig Later

At this point you're ready to play a little. Suppose in one of your chapters he just misses her at a concert. Fine and dandy. But do yourself a favor. Go back a few pages to earlier chapters and write: *Establish both as concert-goers*. This notation will help you two ways. First, the notation will give the chapter another reason for that chapter's existence. Second, the notation will save you from a red face whem, during the scene where he does miss her, you will have to paint yourself *out* of a corner by saying in your novel, "Among other things they had in common was music. That's why they were both at the concert that night." The reader will wonder why, if the fact that they had music in common was important, you waited until the last minute to mention it. Plotting lets you establish facts that you will draw upon later, making your novel seem to the reader to be a beautifully constructed piece of writing.

For instance, suppose you have a chapter well into the book where Herbert gets some money when his aunt dies. If you hadn't established that he had an aunt, and established her earlier, you would be hard-pressed to establish how—at the precise moment he needed cash—an aunt happened to die. So the more notes you make, the merrier. When you get around to writing the book you may not use all of them, but better to have noted than ignored Herbert's aunt. Don't surprise the reader with facts he should have been given soon.

> The bad guys shot bullets at Herbert who, with only a stick in his hand felt helpless. He had no way to defend himself.
> "Land sakes," one of the bad guys shouted. He pointed up to the sky. "Look at her."
> He shouted too late. Hilda, parachuting out of the blue, kicked the bad guys in their noses and made them run away.
> "I forgot to tell you, Herbert," she said, peeking coyly from behind her parachute, "Sky-diving is my hobby."

Herbert—and the reader, too—have every right to be disturbed. Too many such surprises and Herbert will seek another girl. The reader will seek another book. So study those loose-leaf pages with care. Write a sentence on each that tells what the chapter will do. Then, note what preparation should be made in earlier chapters, so the action will be reasonable. If your character needs to know judo, don't give him last minute instructions in the chapter where he must defend himself. A few chapters earlier write a sentence which says you must establish that he takes judo lessons. Some surprises in novels are nice. Too many are deadly.

> "I didn't know you knew sky-diving," Herbert said.
> "I learned when I was in the paratroop," Hilda said.
> "You were in the paratroop?" Herbert said.

"Sure," said Hilda. "I fought side by side with my husband in the last war."
"I didn't know you were married before," Herbert said.
"Eight times," said Hilda.
"Good grief," said Herbert.

Be kind to Herbert and the reader. Don't give them too much to digest at once. Scatter the points through your novel and make them known gradually. A fact here, a fact there, and life will be easier for all. This is why plotting is important. Right, Herbert?

A Word About Flashbacks

You know the routine. Herbert finds that he is gifted with total recall. He hears a sound, smells a smell, or tastes a taste and presto! this reminds him of an incident in the dear, dead days beyond recall which he will recall anyway. Good plotting—the planting of a fact so you can use it later—eliminates useless flashbacks. I do not say that all flashbacks are bad. As Nichols and May said of lepers, "There are good lepers and there are bad lepers; you can't lump them all together." The same applies to the flashback. At times a chapter that takes us back to the past can make sense. But flashbacks, can get out of hand. Plot your chapters with care. Avoid flashbacks. One or two, perhaps, yes, but too many flashbacks and the flashbacks won't do the job. Look at your notes. If every third chapter is a flashback, something's wrong. Better to start your novel at an earlier moment so that the flashbacks won't be flashbacks at all.

Check each page, which represents each chapter, to see if each chapter *does* something. Make certain the forward movement of the plot maintains its momentum. What does that mean? Suppose your rough notes for chapter twelve include the following odds and ends:

1. Action takes place in March
2. Herbert meets Hilda in library by accident. She will have nothing to do with him at first but they almost kiss and make up.
3. Uncle Fuddles appears. Makes hash of possible reconciliation.
4. Establish Hilda as a paratrooper. Needed in chapter fifteen.
5. Establish Herbert as apprentice taxidermist. Needed in chapter thirteen.
6. Establish they both like Faith Baldwin. Needed in final chapter.

Well, to write *that* chapter, which moves the plot along, is no sweat. But on the other hand, suppose your notes for another chapter read:

1. Action takes place in January.
2. Herbert tells Uncle Fuddles about meeting Hilda in used-car lot.
3. Describes scene to Uncle Fuddles, telling how they almost kissed, but Hilda drove off with the used-car salesman.

Disgusted as we may be with Herbert and Hilda because they seem never to get together in time for Christmas, we will be even more disgusted with you as the author. Why didn't you let us see the confrontation between Hilda and Herbert? Why let us hear about it second-hand? The point here is, given two ways to write that chapter, you chose the wrong one. Let the reader in on the action. Don't let him get it by hearsay. Let Herbert do more than recall things. I have no objection to Herbert's talking, but I object when talk replaces action. The scene between Herbert and Uncle Fuddles is not needed. What *is* needed is that scene between Hilda, Herbert, and the used-car salesman. Be efficient. Seek the heart of the matter: the confrontation on the used-car lot. The scene with Uncle Fuddles slows your plot. Nothing happens. Everything in that scene happened somewhere else. Check your notes carefully. Is something happening? Is something *really* happening? And does this thing that happens move the plot along or slow the plot to a grinding halt? Your plotting can tell you. Let it.

A Useful Exercise

Now, just for laughs, in each chapter note the reactions of the characters in that chapter to the chapter's events. To do so is not as foolish as it might sound. When writing the chapter we might get too involved which is all right, because if we didn't get involved, we wouldn't be writers. But getting involved so much that we overlook things we shouldn't is another matter. That's where this plotting helps us. Suppose our friend Hilda meets our friend Herbert by accident in a taxidermy shop. They have both gone there, each without the other's knowledge, to get estimates on stuffing Uncle Fuddles (bunny eyes, optional). Well, we know our friends are on the outs. But do we know how each feels about stuffing Uncle Fuddles? Or, to complete the scenario, do we know how Uncle Fuddles himself feels about it. We may need to know such reaction, we may not, but this early in the game, who can tell? Suppose we note their reactions then, just in case:

> HILDA: Thinks Uncle Fuddles stuffed would be an excellent piece, provided he doesn't clash with the draperies. Bunny eyes? Yes.
> HERBERT: Thinks Uncle Fuddles won't mind, but knows he himself will. Still, everyone else does it these days. Bunny eyes? No.
> UNCLE FUDDLES: To be stuffed and set up as a conversation piece: Hell, no. Who wants to be a hat rack?

What worth do these stray reactions have? Plenty. Every move your characters make and every word they say will reflect the many attitudes your characters possess. Now, while plotting your novel, is the time to list their various reactions to various things. When you're writing that chapter, you might be too involved in writing action to remember these reactions. Remember them here, then, in your outline. Besides, the more of these reactions you list for each character the more that character himself will acquire substance.

Another idea: when you've finished plotting, employ a loose-leaf page for each character. Go through your chapter outlines and copy off his reactions to everything. You will be pleased to discover that, as a bonus, you have a dossier on your cast. Add these extra pages to your notebook filled with the chapter plottings—and you're ahead of the game!

Occasionally, after plotting your novel, you will discover an irritating situation. Chapter eight, which once seemed ideal right where it was, would do better as chapter nine—or even sixteen. Or, you'll find two chapters so identical in content you can't figure how that could be. Don't worry when such things pop up. Be glad to have discovered the weaknesses and inconsistencies in the outline—and not the finished novel. Chapters and chapter ingredients are easier to juggle in outline than in finished products. Rejuggle parts to your heart's content. If this chapter works better there, move it there. If two chapters are alike, study them again. You might wish to combine them into a single chapter. You might wish to keep one and discard the other. Follow your heart.

You are bound to arrive at the moment where you don't know what will happen next. You know how the novel ends, but in another and earlier confrontation, you find no resolution. Let's say Hilda and Herbert have fallen out of an airplane—in chapter seven. They're in for a nasty time when they land. We all know that. They are your main characters. Kill them off in chapter seven and who will kiss under the mistletoe? Don't brood. Don't tear your hair. *Ignore* the mess, assume somehow they survive, and get on with the plotting. Tomorrow or the next day you'll think of a solution. Why stew about it now. Bypass the problem. No writer has *all* the answers when he outlines his novel. Don't be a smartypants and try to be the exception. Plot what you can plot and don't brood about what you can't. Herbert and Hilda will survive. I don't know *how*—at this moment I'm stumped too—but I have faith.

Thus in one fashion or another, with fits and starts, chapter by chapter you plot your novel. You know more about your book now than when your book was only a beautiful dream. Problems have arisen and you have solved them—or, at least most of them. You know your characters better. A few loose ends exist (Hilda and Herbert still falling is one) but time or gravity will take care of things.

Now comes the moment of truth. You re-read your outline, chapter by chapter, and you turn pale. Oh, it's a tremendous outline all right. Lots of action. Stunning characters. It pleases you. But, on the other hand, it doesn't and you realize with a sickening feeling that *not enough* happens. You realize, in panic, that you don't have enough for a novel.

Well, my friend, relax. Don't weep. Don't shoot yourself. Be thankful you discovered the failing of your plot *before* you wrote the dozens and dozens of pages to make your plot into a book. Think of the time plotting has saved you. Better to discover your novel lacks substance now, don't you think? An outline is a matter of days. A novel is a matters of months and seasons.

Now do this. Take your outline and put it away. Go to the beach, if you're a guy, and look at the pretty girls. If you're a girl, buy a hat or bake a cake. Cheer yourself as best you can because you've earned the right. To discover what you have discovered takes courage. We're proud of you. But don't quit. Ever, ever. Promise yourself that tomorrow—the day after at at the latest—you're going to start over, refreshed, work up another outline (perhaps using much of your present one; certainly the characters) and plot a book that *is* a book. You see! Already you're beginning to think like a writer. But let's not dawdle here. Much waits to be written. To start over is no disgrace. To give up —or to complete a book that *isn't* a book—that's the disgrace! It's not only a disgrace, it's a waste of time.

And the more time we waste, the less time we have to go to the beach and see the pretty girls.

Chapter 14

First, But Hardly Final Draft

Time to write two pages a day!

That's what this chapter is about: the *first* draft of your novel. Books, of course, are not written in one sitting. At least, they're not supposed to be. Books are written a chapter at a time. What I suggest here for one chapter will apply to the rest. Agreed? Let's begin.

You have your plot outlined, you know what your book is about, and you know what each chapter must do. You've played with your characters, rounding them out and making them three-dimensional people. You've tinkered with descriptions of settings. You've researched till you're blue in the face. All that remains is to write your book, chapter at a time, two pages a day, rain or shine.

Should you begin at the beginning: the first sentence in the first paragraph? Perhaps. Perhaps not. No slow-motion starts, please. Your first sentence and paragraph must hit the reader where he lives and tell him what the book is about. Makes the idea of writing that first sentence and paragraph awesome, doesn't it? The thought scares the pants off me, too. So when *I* start to write a book, I take the coward's way out. I don't start at the beginning. Who says I have to? I might start halfway through the first chapter, or I might get my feet wet on chapter eight because that chapter has an easy-to-write scene. In the days that follow, as I write elsewhere in my book, I brood about that opening sentence and paragraph. I have plenty of time to brood. After I brood long enough, the right combination of words will present themselves. Then, there's my opening! I might be a hundred pages into the book at that point. Had I waited, pretending to be a Great Artist, I would never have got that far! By bypassing the roadblocks, like the opening of the book, I keep plugging away. You keep plugging away too. On the other hand, if by some wild chance you *do* have that kind of a beginning, begin at the beginning if it pleases you. Later, should you think of an opening that's even more inspired, you can always put it in, can't you? Thanks to your outline, you are not required to begin at the beginning. Begin at the middle, if you like, and work both ways.

That's why the first writing of a book is called the first draft. The first draft is never final. You'll want to tinker with the words, tighten the sentences, perhaps re-noodle the sequence. So recognize your first draft for what it is, the raw and unfinished product that needs much work. In other words, after you've evolved your characters, plotted your plot, and thought about your setting, you simply can't sit down at your typewriter and rip off a masterpiece. Why even use good bond paper for your first draft? Buy the cheapest stock that does the job. Good paper is for typing your final script. Use any first draft that you consider final to start fires. The fire will be hotter than anything you've managed to write. No writer is so good that he can start off—cold—and type out a novel the first time around. Some say they can, but I say that's vanity at work. I suggest their novels would have been even better had they edited and rewritten. Only an amateur or an egomaniac would insult a book publisher by sending him unedited and unrevised copy. I suggest this not to dampen your fervor, but to save you cash. Use the cheapest stock that works—and don't send your first draft off to market.

Write Now, Revise Later

Now, let's assume you've started *somewhere* and your rate is the two pages a day we established earlier. Well, maybe you'll start with the dialogue needed in chapter fifteen. Or maybe you'll start with that tender love scene in chapter six. But when you start, *start*. Keep going. Don't dawdle. Dream when you're away from the typewriter. Keep writing. Keep writing. Keep writing. If the words refuse to come as fast as you'd like them to, make them come. This, believe me, is easier *done* than *said*. Forget that you must write a book. All you must write is *one* sentence, then another, until there you sit with a paragraph finished. Don't stop to admire it. Start the next paragraph. If the prose sings off-key, turn a deaf ear, and keep typing. You have an outline to follow. You *know* what is supposed to happen next in that chapter. But nothing will happen until you write it. So write it and make it happen. Later on, by polishing here and there, your prose will sing a sweet song. What do you care now if the prose mumbles? If you hesitate only for a moment, stop to brood, or even to cry, the momentum is lost. Then, to write those two pages a day you set for yourself will take you several days—and where does that leave you? If, on the other hand, everything you write strikes you as the most beautiful prose ever concocted, don't shout it from the housetop. Don't do anything at all. *Keep writing.* Your judgment may be clouded today. The prose that glitters today will only seem to lie there tomorrow, looking dull. Whether you write winners or losers, keep writing. *That* is the important thing. You can't brood, cheer, and type at the same time. Stay at your typewriter and write—one sentence after another, one paragraph after another. And then, write some more. To write two pages a day is no major burden. Quit moaning. If someone can show you another way, different from mine, that strikes your fancy, cheers, more power to you both. But as long as you're here, write those two pages a day which, I say, is no burden. When I was working eight hours a day at the salt mines, I wrote *my* two pages. In fact, I wrote—at times—ten pages a day. Now, on a clear day, I can average thirty or forty rough pages that, after editing, are distilled down to two or three. You get with it too. Write those two pages, be they good, bad, or indifferent. You can always edit later. You can't edit what you haven't written.

Don't Show Your First Draft To Anyone

After the first day at the typewriter you will be tempted to show someone—anyone!—the deathless prose you have created. Forget this idea fast. The only ones to see and make comments are your family and friends. However charming they are, they are not professional writers or editors, so really, what do they know? Anyway, you don't write to please them. You write to please yourself. Keep your first draft out of the grubby hands of those who love you and wish you well. They might praise you, which is satisfying, but also, they might quibble over this word or that description.

"Well, really! I wouldn't call our street dowdy!"

Or:

"Why don't you have the girl say something else instead of what you've written here? To me, it doesn't read right."

I repeat (coldly but kindly), what do these well-meaning well-wishers know? If they know that much about writing, they should write their own books. They love you, want the best for you, but in the long run, will only confuse you. Later, the same will be true of book critics. Book critics are delightful and well-meaning souls who sometimes don't know any better. If a book critic happens to be a novelist himself he will be unable to divorce his criticism of your novel from the novelist that dwells within him. He will look upon your efforts with favor or disfavor, depending on whether yours is or isn't the kind of book he would or wouldn't, could or couldn't, write. Forgive him. His fault is that he is human, too. If the critic is not a novelist but a paid critic in the hire of some publication. or on the staff of a university, he is a critic pure and simple, but often more simple than pure. If the critic is neither a novelist nor a paid worker, watch out. The critic will either be vicious because this is his one moment of glory or he will heap worthless praise on you and make you think you're better than you are, which, of course, you're not. Don't try to please critic or friend. Please yourself. And when writing your first draft, don't even try to please yourself too much. Like what you write but don't fall in love with each word and comma.

Do Your Own Typing

Some of you will say:

"Listen, I'm not a whiz at typing. I think I'll dictate my book and have my wife transcribe it."

Your typist whoever she might be—wife, daughter, aunt, sister, girlfriend, or that pretty neighbor who can't type her way out of a paper bag—is, I will be the first to admit, a delightful person, salt of the earth, a real pal. Thus, I will be the first to admit that for your typist you couldn't have made a wiser—and more stupid—choice. What I'm saying is, struggle through the first and second *and*, if need be, third draft on your own. Type awkwardly one word at a time, one word every ten minutes if you must, but type it yourself. By the time you've ripped through a dozen pages you will be up to one word a minute and know where the question mark is. Soon after that you'll zip along, perhaps so fast the typewriter will race ahead of your thoughts. Also, you'll know how to work the back-space and the margin release. If the idea of typing frightens you, scribble your draft out in long hand, but under no conditions should you dictate. I have sound reasoning to back this advice.

An author writes for an audience of one: *himself.* You *are* going to pour your heart and soul—the real you we discussed earlier—into this novel, aren't you? If not, why write the novel at all? But to deal with your heart and soul alone with your typewriter is one thing. To place it, edited, on public display, even if the public is only your wife, is another. Instead of trying to please you, the audience of one, you will subconsciously or consciously try to please an audience of two: you and your typist. You will dictate with her reactions in mind. You will water this scene down or dilute that dialogue or change the plot to keep from looking the fool in her eyes. This will not help you get your novel written *right*. Let her read it later if you must. But don't let anyone but you edit your script with a look or a frown.

Be kind to yourself as you type your own first draft. Don't wad up and throw away *anything*. No matter how awful the stuff reads, keep it. Keep every sentence, every paragraph, and every page. Why create a waste basket fire hazard? If you don't like the way a sentence goes, don't rip the paper from you typewriter. Skip down a few spaces, indent, and begin again. Who knows? You might have a grabber of a sentence started. The sentence might not come your way again. Your job in the first draft is to write, not to edit. Write, write, write. Smoke a cigarette and write some more. Maybe you'll be so enthused you won't be able to stop at your two page quota. Cheers. Go ahead. Write four. Write a dozen. Just remember that you also have eight hours to put in at the salt mines, pal. You get paid there. There may be days when it seems you'll never get those two pages written. Gee, that's tough. But stay there. Keep writing. You have a two-page quota to fill before you can waste time feeling sorry for yourself. Don't con yourself by saying: "I'll take off today and do four pages tomorrow."

That kind of tomorrow never rolls around. Write, write, write. On the days you do turn out more than your quota, consider yourself lucky, but don't rest on your oars. Think about what you'll write the next day. Your schedule calls for two pages a day—no matter what. That's what you told your neighbor, wasn't it? Well, two pages a day is the only way you'll get your first draft done on time. Write, write, write. An then, write some more. If, when writing you first draft you don't write a chapter a week at this rate, recheck your sights. Somewhere along the line you are goldbricking. Work. Write, write, write. Who said writers have easy lives?

Revise Chapter By Chapter?

Should you pause to edit and polish each rough chapter before moving on to the next? No. Write your entire book as a rough draft first. Here's why. Suppose your outline calls for this guy to belt that guy, but suppose, also, that when you arrive at this confrontation, your two guys are established as cream puffs. You know instinctively, nobody is going to belt anybody. They will snarl, say mean things, spit, but that will be that. But suppose your plot *needs* the hitting scene? If you polish and edit chapters as you go, thus creating guys who won't hit one another, you'll have to go back, rewrite, edit, and polish some more to change the attitude of your characters. This means the first time you sweated that chapter to final, you sweated in vain. So plunge ahead, write only rough takes on each chapter for your first draft. Keep writing till you reach the end of your novel. To rewrite, edit, or polish one complete rough take is fun. To have to do the job all over again is a waste of time.

As you type onward to the final chapter you will discover what you discovered when you were plotting: this scene or that piece of dialogue works better somewhere else. Thus another reason exists for not editing your first draft to final, chapter by chapter. Why tinker over a chapter to make it crystal clear if, a month later, you have to do that work all over again? Do all your tinkering at once. It's more efficient that way.

What I am about to write here may shock your eighth grade English teacher, but do yourself a favor. Don't make life more complicated than it is. Write your first draft as well as you can, spell the words you know how to spell, and use what you think is correct grammar, *but don't* run to the dictionary every ten minutes to see how to spell a word and *don't* worry about rules of grammar. When you're writing your first draft, you have no time for time-wasting nonsense like that. You are an inspired writer! Your job is to put on paper one word after another! What do you care if *i* comes before *e*, or if the punctuation seems unreal? Allow yourself when writing your first draft, the luxury of genius. Such moments are few and far between. Your moment of genius won't last long, either. Soon now, a sourpuss will look over this prose you created in the heat of genius, cough politely at your syntax, correct your spelling, dot your i's, and make your verbs match your nouns. Who is this sourpuss? The sourpuss will be you, but for the moment, relax. He comes later. You can only do one thing at a time. Now—write. Throw *everything* into your novel. Edit later. Correct later. Be mean later. Be nice now. A good writer—you—can be a good editor—also you—but not, I insist, at the same time. There's a time and place for everything. Your place right now is at your typewriter, writing your rough first draft.

What are you waiting for? Up and at 'em, genius!

Chapter 15

The Second Draft—
Chapter By Chapter

One hundred days—or less—have passed. Somehow or other, there it sits: your first draft! You wrote it in one fell swoop from start to finish. You didn't worry about spelling, grammar, description, the rightness of the dialogue, or the aptness of the action. You simply wrote ten pages—or more—to a chapter, letting those pages carry your plot forward. You didn't look back to see if you had a winner or a loser. That's the way we geniuses are, wouldn't you say?

Now bring out the first draft, brace yourself, and prepare to look back. Prepare to read it, chapter by chapter, and tinker. This tinkering will result in your second draft.

Let's assume that each chapter, hot from your typewriter, is ten pages long. Fine and dandy, but the chapters contain many useless paragraphs, words, and sentences. When you eliminate these you might end with six or—frightening thought!—only four pages per chapter instead of the ten your novel needs. That's one reason the second draft is a lifesaver. The second draft will be your insurance against a chapter, edited to its vitals, vanishing because it has no vitals.

A Checklist to Follow

Here's the way I work on the second draft. This method might work for you, too. We are both concerned with these questions:

1. Does the chapter do what the outline requires?
2. Even if it does, does the chapter contain enough action?

3. And is there dialogue enough to break the visual monotony of too many straight paragraphs?
4. Where can the present action be amplified?
5. Where will additional dialogue fit best?
6. Should the chapter contain more description?

But even before these basic questions, there are general questions new writers sometimes ask, like: how long should a chapter be? Abraham Lincoln said a man's legs should be long enough to reach the ground. Let us say that a chapter should be long enough to do its job. But bear in mind we face pitfalls. Chapters can always be too long. Seldom can they be too short. Chapters are not arbitrary divisions. There are good reasons for chapter breaks, but some new writers ignore them, making their novels one terribly long chapter. Bad. Other new writers use mathematics and not logic. Come hell or high water, every ten pages they start a new chapter. Bad. A chapter, I say, is a unit, a *fairly complete* unit. A chapter can't, however, be a totally independent unit; it relies on other chapters for its strength.

One way to see where chapters should begin and end is to look upon each scene in your novel as a chapter by itself. If Hilda and Herbert are smooching on the high-wire, that's one scene. Thus, that's one chapter. Why blend that scene with a scene in which their fathers, in another town, are discussing dowery. Let the fathers have their own scene and chapter too.

Now, having concluded that "one scene equals one chapter," let's see where this rule will not apply. Suppose Herbert goes from butcher shop to butcher shop in search of hamhocks for his lady fair, but ends up with pigs' feet instead. That total sequence, according to our outline, is what the chapter is about. As the poor dolt goes from butcher shop to butcher shop, should we make each encounter a separate chapter? No. Apply common sense here. The "scene" in this instance is his visit to *all* the butcher shops. Have we broken the rule so soon? Not quite. We have, though, bent it a little.

There are other instances where "one scene equals one chapter" could make us look ridiculous: the courtroom scene, for instance. The scene, which is the full trial, goes on and on and on. To insist that the entire proceedings be one chapter will give us a long. long chapter. So we do this. Instead of making it one continuous scene (and thus one long, long chapter) we use each confrontation as a separate and distinct scene or chapter. In this chapter the lawyer questions Witness A. In the next chapter the other lawyer cross-examines Witness A. Witness B has the luxury of his own chapter, and so do the others. Since the lawyers each try to establish a point with each witness, to give each confrontation its own chapter makes sense, doesn't it? The same would apply to the living room scene that goes on and on. Or the beach-house scene. Or two on a see-saw. Each confrontation is a new chapter. When a new character enters, let him have a chapter to himself. If Siamese twins enter, common sense should prevail; let them share a chapter.

Where Does a Chapter Start?

We could sum up this way: when trying to figure where to start and stop a chapter, first see if one scene will serve our needs as one chapter. If not, perhaps a collection of scenes, with the same premise (seeking hamhocks), will do the job. If that doesn't work, look upon each confrontation within a scene as a confrontation that merits its own chapter. And if that doesn't work, ask a friendly policeman. The point is, a chapter, though technically a complete unit, is not actually a complete unit because it alone is not a complete story. Each chapter has its roots in the chapter before it and its problems resolved in the chapters that follow.

Remember those old movie serials, like *The Perils of Pauline*? They were called cliff-hangers, and with good reason. Each filmed episode, however satisfying, left the audience unsatisfied. Pauline might have been saved from the sawmill's saw, but when the episode ended, there she was, hanging over a cliff. The movie fan returned the following week to see her get out of that mess only to see her tied to the railroad track, here comes the train, and TO BE CONTINUED! Chapters should end with cliff-hangers too. These can be subtle—but not *too* subtle,—or they can be stem-winders. True, the place to resolve the plot of your novel is the final chapter, but en route minor problems can be solved: saving Pauline from the oncoming train, the cliff, the killer whale, or the sex-mad bingo player. Make sure, though, that having solved a minor problem, a major one still bubbles, because the major problem is what your novel is about. Look over your chapter endings for cliff-hangers.

> "I'm glad," said Hilda, "that you hit the robber in the nose. He was going to do me great harm."
> "What I did was nothing," said Herbert. "Now that we are safe, let's kiss a little."
> "But here comes a wild elephant," she said.
> "Good grief," said Herbert. "What'll we do!"

If *that* doesn't get the reader to the next chapter where, waiting for him is dialogue that will make him read on, nothing will.

Thank Goodness for Scissors Because They Are *Handy Gadgets*

Scissors allow you to hack your chapter apart, making jigsaw puzzle pieces of blocks of dialogue and paragraphs of description. You can reassemble these items into any order that strikes your fancy—with no wasted rewriting involved. You'll want to use a stapler, and no glue, to fasten these odds and ends together. Staples are better than glue because glue is not only messy but final. You can unstaple sections you can't unglue. If you cut a paragraph from the middle of a page, staple the remaining sections together right away. Otherwise you might forget which goes where. Insert the hacked away paragraph into the new position by cutting the new page apart, dropping in the paragraph, banging the stapler a few times, and there you are: *instant* revision!

After you have a new beginning stapled into some of your chapters and new endings tacked on where needed, see what else you can do to make each chapter more effective as well as a few pages longer, so that when you edit, you'll have ten pages left.

Can The Reader See What You See?

Although it is difficult to do because you wrote every word yourself, read each chapter with care and as objectively as you can. Consider the physical setting—where the action takes place. Have you established the time of day? You can picture the setting, but can the reader? A room is more than four walls. It possesses a mood. But have you said this in so many words? Does the setting, as real settings do, appeal to the senses of the reader? Does a setting like the Golden Hotdog Grill, for example, smell of hamburgers, onions, disinfectant, or roses? Is it dimly lighted—or bright as a Chinese restaurant? What of the booth where Hilda and Herbert are: is it comfortable in a leathery way or is it a hard wooden seat? Does the jukebox play? If so, what kind of music: hillbilly, rock-&-roll, or Muzak? Perhaps there is a live combo? What kind: rock, hillbilly, chamber, or the kind of cocktail music, that all sounds like "April in Paris" or "Manhattan Serenade." Do street noises come through the door and, if so, what are they: church bells or the traffic cop's tweet. In your first draft, chances are you could visualize the setting exactly, but did you write the setting so the reader could visualize it, too? If not, do something here and now. Rectify that. Read your chapters with the settings foremost in your mind. Have you milked each setting for all its worth? Can the reader, as you can, smell, feel, taste, and hear it? Make sure. Your task at this point, the second draft, is not to delete but to add. For now, put everything in your novel. The more you add to each chapter, the more you will have later from which to pick and choose. So don't be shy. Add paragraphs here, there, and everywhere. Describe the places we find Hilda, heighten her mood, or deepen her character. Hack away with scissors to insert gems. You will soon lose track of how many "rough" pages you do have. What with lifting this paragraph from here and making that page short, you have added several paragraphs to another page, making it two feet long. No matter. In the final typing your script will look neat. In your first and second drafts, neatness doesn't count. The prize you seek is clarity.

Now, read your chapters again from another viewpoint: dialogue. Is there too much here and not enough there? To solve the problem of too much here, break the dialogue with a brief paragraph of description or interior monologue by the main character. But if there is too much dialogue of another kind—one person rambling on and on, take drastic action. Turn long speeches into quick debates, show reactions, and your novel will read faster and be more true to life. Later, when you edit, you can tighten the dialogue to make it more efficient, but in the interim, you've added extra pages. Now you can hack away, skim the cream from the surface (to mix a metaphor), and end with ten pages per chapter. But at that point your ten pages will be more telling that the ten pages of your first draft.

Now look again at your chapters, and concentrate this trip on those paragraphs of description. Do they seem to run on and on, paragraph after paragraph. Then break them by inserting dabs of dialogue: maybe one comment, maybe several, just so your reader doesn't see anything but solid blocks of description as far as the eye can see. Add new dialogue and staple it in. Or add some of the dialogue you've cut out elsewhere.

You're about finished with the second draft. Give your manuscript one final reading and be mean. Does each chapter do what your plot demands—or does the chapter ramble? Your chapters each have the responsibility of carrying the plot forward, step by step. Only when you are positive (cross your heart and hope to die) that each chapter does the work cut out for it should you stop working on the second draft. If a chapter is heavy on description and light on action, this is the time to type a few pages of action and staple them in. You are closer to your script than any reader or editor will be. Thus, you will see things they won't—or that they can't unless you spell every detail out. That's why you must be mean to yourself. If your chapters are not crystal clear—tinker with them. Finally, if all the chapters—that stapled-together mess—don't do everything as a team, your book is not efficient. Rework it. Add, but don't subtract. This is the draft in which you add to your book. The next draft is the one you will hate.

On the third draft most of your gems bite the dust.

Chapter 16

Ouch! The Art of Self-Editing

The third draft—this one—is where you edit. Sorry about that.

Although there is no way to make editing painless, does it help to know that some editing is not as painful as other editing? No matter. By now you have written sentences that are gems and you are secretly in love with them. You have written, also, sentences which were gems at the time you wrote them but now make you rather ill. You can't wait to edit them into oblivion, but still you are consumed by an overwhelming reluctance to throw away a single word. This makes sense. Words are hard to come by. To toss them out seems a sin. All writers feel this way, so you are not alone. Thus, when you edit paragraphs, sentences, and words into oblivion, expect to feel pain. I refuse to be a Doctor Spock and offer you reassurance. Doctor Spock consoles human beings who, at times, left to their own devices, can heal themselves. Your manuscript won't. You have to edit the mess. These are the facts of a writer's life and I refuse to con you by saying that to edit is easy. To edit is not easy. To edit is not easy. There, I've said it again.

Save your moans for later. Let's edit this thing you look upon as a novel, but which, at this stage, is not a novel at all. At this stage your manuscript is little more than a stack of stapled-together chapters that contain much unmitigated babbling with, here and there, to break the monotony and make me proud of you, streaks of writing that sing. Our task now is to make every page, sentence, and word sing. If they don't, out they go!

Once Straight Through

But why should we bother to edit paragraphs or even pages that will be discarded? Do that and we'd waste time. So do this. Start with chapter one and read to the last sentence in the last chapter. The ten-page chapters, as the result of the second draft, have been beefed up to chapters that contain fifteen or more pages. Now is the time to trim fat. Get yourself a *yellow*—not black, red, green, blue, or purple—marking pencil. Why yellow? Because when you come across a word, sentence, or paragraph you don't need, you'll mark it out with your yellow marker. If you use any other color, especially black, the edited-out words or phrases will be lost forever from sight. With a yellow marker you can still read what you have crossed out. Later you might wish to reinstate the words there or somewhere else. Why kill them dead? What we're doing first in the third draft, before worrying about grammar, is trimming the fat from the novel. So be cruel. Mark out anything and everything that fails to move your plot forward. That paragraph you labored over, the one that describes the sunset over the used-car lot, is sheer poetry, isn't it? But does it make the plot move on? No? Would, perhaps, a sentence suffice? No? Eliminate. Now, go on to the next paragraph which contains several gems you feel should be bronzed. Unfortunately each gem paraphrases the other, doesn't it? Why waste the reader's time to tell of three different ways Hilda feels anger? Her anger only happens one way at that moment. Choose the gem that's most accurate and get rid of the rest.

Tackle your dialogue the same hateful way. Is *all* that talk essential? Couldn't Hilda and Herbert have reached the same point in three speeches instead of ten? In real life, dialogue cannot be edited and is not efficient. But in your novel, dialogue can be edited and made efficient. Kill some of those wonderful speeches. Get rid of this and that exchange. Let your characters speak efficiently. Don't you wish real people could speak that way?

While you're hacking your writing, humor me. Take your yellow marker and edit out nearly every adjective and adverb you can find. Common sense will tell you when *not* to do this. If your sentence reads, "Hilda *angrily* stomped from the room," your sentence would read better, "Hilda stomped from the room." On the other hand, if you sentence reads, "Hilda gave Henry a *black* eye," or "Her dress was *red,*" common sense tells you to let well enough alone or your sentences will lose meaning. But in most instances, edit adjectives and adverbs out. You're using that yellow marker. Later, if you like, humor yourself, and reinstate the words. I have a feeling, though, once out, many of the words will stay out for keeps. You will find you have—with this one method—made your writing more efficient. The final choice is up to you, of course, but in this editing orgy humor me and give adjectives and adverbs the ax.

Is This Scene Effective?

Be the cruelest editor in captivity. Demand that each scene carry its own weight. If the scene doesn't, sigh if you like, but out it goes. There's *this* consolation I can offer you. You won't have to worry about polishing the grammar of a scene that isn't there. Does the thought console you? Probably not, but get rid of the scene anyway.

Thus with your yellow marker, plow through your novel, page at a time, eliminating scenes you don't need, and words you don't need. If you are brave, you'll leave behind you a wide yellow swath and have, when done, chapters which once ran fifteen pages reduced to ten again. On the other hand, if you're gutless, you will have eliminated nothing, in which case I don't suggest you send your script to a publishing house. Don't expect an editor there to do the work they pay you as the author to do. No need to send them a thing because you will not have written a novel. You will have only put some words on paper, something anyone can accomplish. Writers not only create sentences that are gems, but know when to throw some of the gems away.

Before we brood about spelling—a subject I have such a pet theory on that editors panic—let's tackle the edited manuscript again, this time being alert for:

1. Present participles
2. Loose and periodic sentences
3. The word "very"

4. Paragraphing
5. Obscenities
6. And that awful word "it"

Get that look out of your eyes. We'll learn as we go. On this trip through your novel, forget about its beauty and look upon each sentence as a separate unit. To go over your script with a fine-tooth comb is not, I assure you, as complicated as it sounds.

The Omnipresent Participle

First, there's this business of the present participle. You may, or may not, agree, but do me another favor since you've humored me this far. Get rid of as many present participles as you can. These are the words that end with *ing.*

> She was *running.*
> They were *laughing.*
> *Being* happy, she hiccuped.
> The *meandering* stream was beautiful.
> The *giggling* girl looked ridiculous.

These *ing* words are all right, but they lack strength. Sentences should make statements—simple and fast. This allows the reader to go on to the next sentence, and the next. Present participles—these *ing* words—slow a sentence, render it less vital, and rob it of power. Call me a fuddy-duddy but I stamp out nearly every present participle I can. Thus, *my* version of the above sentences would be:

> She *ran.* And isn't that quicker to read than *running?*
> They *laughed.* Same thing!
> *She was so happy,* she hiccuped. Good old cause and effect.
> The stream *meandered* and was beautiful. Better? I think so.
> *The girl giggled.* She looked ridiculous. When you have two thoughts of equal value, two sentences are better than one.

But to me, the real trouble with present participles, those flabby words that end in *ing,* is that they make us lazy. To write *she was run-*

ning is more natural than to write *she ran*. But *she ran* makes the present participle *running* a vigorous word. Wherever you see a present participle, look around. Chances are in the same neighborhood you'll see a form of the verb *to be*. I'll agree that *I am, you are,* and *he is* are nice, but at times they say less than they should. *I am laughing* is the slowpoke way of saying *I laugh*. Check the verb *to be* when the verb has a present participle for a friend and see how, if possible, you can rework the sentence to break up the friendship. For instance, *to be* can be dreary even when a present participle is not around. *To be* can be replaced by a verb with more guts. *She was beautiful* becomes *she possessed beauty*. *The house was creaky* becomes *the wind made the house creak*. She was *crying* (there's the present participle sneak*ing* in) becomes *she cried* or *the sight of Bill made her cry* which is even better. In other words, don't let things happen and report the result. *Make* things happen. Cause the effect. *This* causes *that* to happen. *This* doesn't happen by itself. And get rid of present participles where you can. Do you find the thought appealing? Or, does the thought appeal?

While you tinker with the verbs of each sentence, check their lineage to see if the verbs match the nouns. We all know, I presume, that *I is* is poor English and so is *I are*. *I am* sounds better, doesn't it? *They is* shows that you are a clod whereas *they are* shows you got through the fifth grade. Trickiest are those sentences that meander: subjects get so far removed from the verb that the two can't see one another through the syntax. Check these kinds of sentences with care. Mentally erase all clever asides (called clauses) and reduce in your mind the sentence to its bare bones: subject and verb. Is the subject plural and the verb singular? Fix. And while you fix, sort out the sentence. Make it two or three sentences instead of one. After all, the less complicated the sentence, the less chance of errors in grammar. Long and involved sentences not only confuse the writer but can confuse the reader, too. He doesn't read novels to sort out your syntax.

Why give yourself added grief? Don't make a sentence *do* too much. Check each sentence you wrote. Is each a hodgepodge of side thoughts, or does the sentence possess a central message? Sentences can never be too short. They can always be too long. If we lose our way in long sentences, readers will lose their way, too. Never use one sentence where two or more sentences will do. Keep your sentences simple. To break the monotony now and then, use a longer sentence if you must, but don't make a habit of that sort of thing.

As you edit your script, look for loose sentences. These aren't sentences that can fall off the page. These are sentences that speak their piece, say what they have to say, and then, keep rambling on. Such sentences could be ended before the last word by putting a period (.) in the sentence earlier.

The opposite of a loose sentence is the periodic sentence. A periodic sentence doesn't have its full say until the period.

> Because her old man is rich, I love that chick.

Stop *that* sentence before the period and you won't have much of a sentence. "Okay," you say, "but so what?"

Just this. You have plotted your book so it moves—efficiently—from start to finish. The last chapter is essential. It wraps up the story. Your task has been to make the reader move from one chapter to the next. But before you can accomplish that, you must make him go from one sentence to the next. If he doesn't, he'll not finish the chapter and not finish the book. A periodic sentence—and a good plot—are the best tools you have to carry the reader along. Each sentence you write is a complete thought, but you don't allow the reader to know the complete thought until he has reached the end of the sentence. By that time, his eyes take in the next few words of the next sentence, whetting his interest you hope, and there he goes again, riding another periodic sentence, one to the next, sentence after sentence.

That, oversimplified, is the beauty of the periodic sentence. Of course, if the words in the sentence—or the thought in the sentence—are dull, he'll put the book aside regardless. But periodic sentences can help. I'd suggest you use some in your novel. Reconstruct your sentences with simple editing. Move clauses and phrases to the front of the bus. Or break the sentence down and uncomplicate it. Make two or three sentences out of one. You don't, of course, make every sentence periodic. Your reading "ear" will tell you when to ease off.

The "Very" Thing

Now let's move to a very important item: *very*. Each time you come across *very* in your script, do away with the word—fast. *Very* is a word that lazy writers use. To such writers, water is never scalding, but very hot; the blonde is never filled with glee, but very happy; and the day does not last forever; the day is only very long. Frankly, the one time I approve of *very* is when you shoot a *Very* pistol. Any other time you use *very*, shoot yourself instead. *Very* is at once a handy—and ridiculous—word. *Very* is supposed to heighten the words it modifies. *Very*, as pointed out, makes hot things hotter, happy blondes happier, and long days longer. But I suggest that whenever you employ *very* to strengthen a word, you chose the wrong word in the first place. Take a hard look at every word that *very* must make stronger. Then, throw that word away, throw *very* away, and find a word that is more apt. In dialogue, perhaps, *very* might belong, but never, never, never does *very* belong anywhere else. I'm very sure of that.

Adverbs ad nauseum

Your book at this moment probably contains many adverbs. Adverbs, for the most part, are useless words we use to make verbs sound better. If *very*, which is an adverb, is sloppy writing, an over-abundance of other adverbs is even sloppier writing. You might not feel this way, but *I* do. I hate adverbs. Now and then, some will slip through, but mostly, I look upon adverbs as willy-nilly words. Adverbs are used when the writer is too lazy to find a verb more apt. He hides the weakness of the verb with a smoke-screen labeled adverb.

She shouted huskily. What nonsense. *Her shouts were husky*, is better. Thus *husky* has value. *Husky* is not a vague after-thought. *She ran quickly*. Stupid. How else *could* she run? If she didn't run quickly, she would walk. Don't even try to clean up such messes. Edit out *quickly* and feel better. I know *I* will. *She whispered tearfully*. Soggy. Better to say *as she whispered, tears came to her eyes*. If tears are important, give them the importance they deserve, Don't dilute their value with an adverb. *Angrily, she ran home.* Break this sentence into two sentences. *She was angry. She ran home.* Or, be clever. Use semi-colons: *she ran home; she was angry.* In any event, death to most adverbs!

Watch "It!"

Get rid of *it! It* messes your clarity and makes hash of *it.* Clara Bow was the *It* Girl, teenagers feel out of *it,* and yesterday *it* rained. In other words, *it* is a vague pronoun that can lead to trouble. Besides, *it* isn't efficient. Go through your manuscript and give each *it* the third degree. See if *it* does the job you want *it* to. Used the right way, *it* can have value. Used the wrong way *it* can get you in a peck of trouble. Once I wrote the sentence *He took a cigar from his pocket and lit it.* Lit what? The cigar? The pocket? *It* should take the place of the last noun that precedes *it.* So, watch *it! It was a cold rain. What* was a cold rain? Better to write, *the rain was cold.* In one fell swoop you eliminate *it* and, by giving the adjective a better position in the sentence, you make your adjective work harder. *It was sad* becomes *the day was sad;* and, even more telling, *she felt left out of it all* becomes *she was lost and lonely.*

From *it* we move to *its* and *it's. Its* is a possessive pronoun. *It's* is a contraction. *Its* comes in handy when a ship loses *its* rudder. *It's* comes in handy, I suppose, when we don't want to take the time to write out *it is,* but since we're getting rid of *it* where we can, you shouldn't let *it* trouble you.

Lets and *let's* are foolers, too. *Lets* is a verb and nothing more: *I let the cat out, you let the cat out, he lets the cat out. Let's* is a contraction which translates into *let us.* Thus we have *let's let the cat out,* or: *let us let the cat out.*

We approach the business of possessives. Here we use, mostly, the *'s.* To make the noun possessive, the *'s* comes in handy. Put the apostrophe before the *s.* If the noun is plural put the apostrophe after the *s. My daughter's lipstick* means *the lipstick of my daughter,* but *my daughters' lipstick* means *the lipstick of all my daughters.* What if a singular word like *dress* ends in an *s?* Dealer's choice. Some say the *dress's color* and other says the *dress' color.* The plural of *dress* is *dresses.* The *dresses' color* looks better than the *dresses's color* which, looks like the spelling of Mississippi. Possessive pronouns don't need *'s. This house is theirs,* not *this house is their's or her's or hi's.*

Those Famous Anglo-Saxon Words

Let's now consider obscenities. If your novel contains obscenities, ride herd on them. Don't let them ride herd on you. You will accuse me, and rightly so, of being a Puritan because I don't care for novels that contain dirty words. I will be the first to admit, in rebuttal, that times *do* exist when obscenity is essential: when you hit your thumb with a hammer or when your wife dents the fender of the car. But you can't hammer your thumb or brood about a fender while you're writing your novel, can you, so why have obscenities on every page? I myself employ them now and then, usually in dialogue, but not often. Being a Puritan has nothing to do with the subject. I don't use dirty words for a practical reason: dirty words have become so common-place they have lost shock value. If you use them to shock your reader, don't. The poor reader is exposed to enough dirty words in one day to last him a lifetime. Would-be novelists scribble dirty words on billboards, sidewalks, walls, and in the dust on the tail-gates of trucks. I suppose these would-be novelists are attempting to communicate, too, but their method leaves much to be desired and their plotting at best is scanty. To write and run away is not easy. No one stays around long enough to write a paragraph these days.

Your reader is so used to dirty words that to find them in a novel strikes him as an everyday event. Let him read a novel that has no dirty words and he might be pleasantly surprised.

Another obscenity is spelling. As you edit your script you should pay attention to how you spell words. Don't spell them so they look too funny. Editors like scripts that contain correctly-spelled words and so do the readers. Most of us can spell most words, other words trip us up, but if a way exists that will make better spellers of some of us, I've yet to find the secret. I have blind spots. I'm sure you do, too. Others can spot our spelling errors, but not us. Why is that? I know there exist words that I will never learn to spell at all. I avoid these when I can. For me to look them up in the dictionary is a waste. As soon as I need the word again, out must come the dictionary again. I've not remembered. For instance, I'm never certain how to spell *embarrassed*. No matter how many *r*'s and *s*'s I use, the word doesn't look right. Words that end in *ize* and *ise* bewilder me. Was I sick that day in school the teacher explained when to use which? Is the word *recognized* or *recognised*? Do you *hypnotize* a person or *hypnotise*? None of the characters in my novels go through *adolecense*, or *adolesence*, whatever the spelling is. They go through puberty, which is the best I can offer them. The fault is not theirs. The fault is mine. I simply can't spell certain words. Does this help you in your hour of need? No? Well, go through your novel and check every word for spelling, the words you don't know how to spell, and the words you think you do. Use a dictionary. You'll not catch every error so don't expect to. I don't catch all mine. Sometimes I don't even try. This attitude of mine might shock you, but know this, it shocks editors more. But I refuse to be *embarassed* or *embarrassed* or however that word is spelled. I take the philosophic view. Some people can't roller-skate, some people can't play chess, and I reserve the right to mispell, or is it misspell? There! We have discussed spelling. I promised that we would.

By this time your manuscript will look like something the cat dragged in. Globs of writing will have been edited out by your yellow marker. Sentences will have been tightened or revised. New words will be scrawled in over edited-out ones. This sentence, perhaps, will move elsewhere. In other words, your script is intelligible only to you. Don't worry. This is always the case. To give you the full idea of what hash we can make of our own writing, I offer you the first few paragraphs of this book's chapter one. Only *I* would wade through and make sense of the litter. (See illustration, page 124.)

You see sentences moved about. You see words replacing others. You see loose sentences turned into periodic sentences. You see phrases eliminated because they slow the action. You won't see many adjectives and adverbs edited out because at this stage of the writing game I don't put them in often. You will see where one word takes the place of several. For instance,one sentence read at first:

> If everyone of you who will "someday write a book" were to write it and ship it
> out to the publisher, chances are there'd be a lot of good books better than mine
> on the market and I'd be out of business in an instant.

By trimming the fat, that hodge podge became:

> The thought that this horde might someday write those books should frighten
> me. Certainly many would be better than mine. I'd be out of business—fast.

What I did, you can do. Check your novel sentence by sentence. Make hash of your novel—and from that hash let clarity come. Then put your writings aside and take a few days off. You've almost finished your final draft. But you need time away from the book. You are too familiar with its innards. When you read one sentence you can anticipate the next. You have your novel memorized. To review at this point, without a breather, would be ridiculous. Make haste slowly. Take your time, especially here. You are near the Moment of truth. Go see a movie. Cut grass. Go fishing. Make curtains. Do anything for a few days—or weeks—but don't think about your script. Forget, if you can, that your book exists.

Then, after that sabbatical, pick up the mutilated pages and read your book from start to finish. Your detachment will not last long, but what else can we do? Read swiftly. Stop to make minor editing repairs if you like but no major overhauls permitted this trip. Pretend you're not the author. Pretend you're reading the book for the first time. You'll be, I hope, surprised at what you've done.

You might, vain you, murmur, "It's the greatest." Or you, too critical you, say, "It drags in spots." You might want to heighten this sequence or tighten that one. Fine and dandy. Do it. Your script looks like hash anyway. Make more hash of it. Use scissors. Edit till your heart breaks. Then, edit some more. Rewrite this scene. Rewrite that chapter. Throw out description. Throw in description. Move dialogue

FIRST CHAPTER

the Club is / must be

(12)

So You ~~want~~ [re going] to write a novel?

← Welcome to the club! ~~It's a~~ whopper ~~because~~

~~I think the people~~ who are "~~going~~ [plan] to write that book someday"
~~actually~~ did form a club, ~~the~~ national convention would include
two out of ~~every~~ three ~~persons in the country.~~ [Thought should] This frightens
me ~~at times~~ as ~~it frightens any~~ free-lance writer who turns out
ordinary fare. If everyone ~~one of you who~~ "~~will someday write a~~
book" were to write ~~it, ship it to the~~ publisher, ~~chances are~~ [free] [his book]
there'd be ~~a lot of good~~ books [better] than mine ~~on the market~~ and
[don't] I'd be out of business, ~~in an instant.~~ But ~~as it is,~~ I'm ~~not refuse to~~
~~in~~ panick. ~~I happen to like books and I happen to like writers~~
~~of books.~~ If you write a book [better] ~~than I write one, so be it,~~
congratulations. I ~~must write just~~ [IF I CAN'T WRITE BETTER] harder or ~~I~~ deserve
[the treadline] [selfishly] ~~to fall by the wayside. That's why~~ I'm pleased you ~~are going~~ [plan]
to write ~~your novel.~~ [because] You ~~might~~ make a better writer ~~out of~~ me.
[ACTUALLY] In the interim, let me ~~pass along a few~~ [OFFER SOME] tricks of the [writing] [stet]
trade, a trade that I am ~~still trying~~ [seek] to master [myself.] ~~Where~~
~~writers are concerned,~~ [all] None of us have the answers. If we ~~had~~ did
[only] we would write ~~nothing~~ but best-sellers, ~~in reality. Writers~~ [and we certainly don't do that]
[when Write] ~~helping~~ writers is ~~another example of~~ [it] the blind leading the blind.
~~If Accept~~ [you] whatever I ~~take~~ in this book as gospel, [do it] ~~only~~ on the
condition that you ~~have~~ [can] ~~right to write gospel, and I~~ [too] do.
~~Fair enough?~~

In this book I ~~am going to~~ [can only] suggest one ~~way~~ [method] to write ~~a~~ [your] novel.
~~This is~~ [is my way a roaring success?] the way I write ~~mine.~~ ~~And in writing them this way.~~
[N's] [Does that help?]
I've sold four in two years. ~~They are not~~ ~~earthshaking novels~~
~~but~~ I'm proud of them,---and as jazz men say, they keep me in bread

Keep me on my toes and

around. Then—STOP!

Stop cold!

Put away your scissors, stapler, and marker. For better or for worse, your novel *is* finished.

Do you recall at the start of this effort that you had to stop talking about writing and start writing? The same advice applies here. You could tinker with your novel till hell freezes over. The tinkering, the editing, the additions, the subtractions, and the extra thought might make your novel better. But if you are ever to get a novel published, sooner or later you have to stop tinkering, type the final script on good white bond paper, and send the novel off to the market place. The coward's way out, at times, is to keep tinkering. Bah humbug! All I know is, I could still be revising my first book. But if I were the script would still be here in my typewriter and the three other novels would not be published, either. I am the first to admit that no one writer can polish *too* much. Only ask yourself this: do you have one book in you, or two—or three? You can't start the second till you finish the first. Think that over!

Don't feel you're through editing, though. As you type your own final copy (which you can do because by now you're a typing whiz) you will find yourself inserting a word here and a sentence there. For the moment, just make sure each sentence has a verb, a period at the end, and there you are. Don't use periods for commas, be kind to your dog, and look both ways when you cross the street. While you're on the other side of the street, buy a copy of *Elements of Style* (Macmillan) by William Strunk, Jr., and E. B. White. You can read the book in one sitting, and the book is better than a college education. The book will teach you more grammar than any human should learn, and—happily——one thing the book doesn't do is teach you how to spell.

The third draft is completed. You've done the best you could. That's all anyone could ask of you. Whether you've done well enough is another question. You'll not know that until you type your book on good bond paper and send it to market. So now we must kick your book out of the house. That is what the last chapter is about: ways to improve your kicking.

Chapter 17

Your Finished Novel—
Where to Send It

Whew!

Your script waits to be typed—*final*. But a thousand questions, which is an exaggeration, need answers. How should you type it? What of copyright? Do you need an agent? Suppose the movies buy your book? Up to this point you have been too involved in writing the novel to think of these matters, or let us suppose that you have. Now let's look at matters which have nothing to do with writing your novel, but have to do with the whys and wherefores of selling it.

First, what of preparing the manuscript? *Type* it—doublespaced with regular upper and lower case type—on some kind of good *white* bond paper. Don't write it out longhand for two reasons: one, the writing will be hard to read; and two, your fingers might fall off. Use regular typewriter type—pica or elite. Don't use those fancy type faces that look like handwriting or italics. Teenage girls use those to write love notes. The poor editor who will eventually read your novel has a hard enough time as things are, wading through his quota of unsolicited manuscripts. Why make him blind before his time? Type on one side of the page only. As long as you're typing, make not one but two carbon copies. A sound reason exists for those two carbons. If (happy day!) a publisher wants to publish your novel, one of the first things he will call for is a carbon copy. He needs the carbon because while one end of the publishing house drools over the magnificence of your prose, the other end of the house tries to figure how to make your manuscript into a book: how many pages, what size type, and what weight paper? If you type just one carbon copy and don't send it, or if you have typed no copy at all, you will have to pay for the publisher to run an extra copy. Tedious task, what? Not much, but money is money, so why not make two carbons? Then when the publisher requests one, send him one. The other? Keep that around in case there is a big train robbery and Robin Hood makes off with the script.

What about the title of your book? No matter how strongly you may feel about your own choice, the publisher usually has equally strong ideas about what will sell. Listen to his suggestions. He's had some experience.

So there you sit, becalmed, with neat piles of paper in front of you: one pile for the original, and two other piles which are the carbon copies of your book. What next? Well, tuck the carbons—both sets—away in a safe place until they are needed. At first you have only to worry about the original which sits in all its glory. How do you send the manuscript to market? There are two ways. Both are acceptable. One, though, is more efficient than the other. Let's look at both. The first way—the efficient way—is not to send the entire manuscript. Send a few chapters—certainly the first, last, and whichever others you consider stem-winders—plus a one-page (no more than that, please!) synopsis which tells the plot of your book. Don't make your synopsis a cliff-hanger. *Tell* the plot. Editors have trouble enough without being required to guess how stories end. Ship the few selected chapters to the publishing house of your choice. Simple as that. Why is this more efficient? To read a few chapters and a synopsis takes less time to read than an entire book. Anyway, no editor worth his salt will read a complete book, word for word, unless the book strikes his fancy. He will sample the writing. So make life easy for the poor soul. Your synopsis tells him instantly what your plot is. The few chapters show your writing ability. Best, this method is the same as looking over the editor's shoulder. You are saying: "If you think chapter ten is a knee-slapper, read chapter fifteen."

Mailing A Few Chapters Saves Time

By sending a few chapters and a synopsis you put your best foot—chapters, that is—forward. If the editor likes what he reads, he will request the rest. But if he doesn't, back your script will come—and in less time than it would have taken him to read and reject the entire book. I estimate that a completed manuscript can visit one publishing house in the time a few chapters plus outline can visit several.

The other method, of course, is to dump the entire shooting match on an editor's desk. Either way is all right. The first way seems to me more efficient.

Under no conditions should you send the book to two or more publishers at the same time. To do so is as foolish as asking two girls to marry you. Suppose they both say yes? To have two publishers hot for your novel doesn't put you in a better position to bargain. The publishing world is not like that. Just as the fellow who proposes to two girls might end with none, you might end with both houses saying to hell with you. They would phrase it more politely, but the message would be the same.

Can you copyright your script before you send it out? Not easily— that's my answer. Copyright laws allow you to copyright unpublished plays, but books and short stories, no. The only way to secure a copyright on a novel prior to publication is for you, yourself, to publish it— that is, reproduce the book by some mechanical means—mimeograph, etc. Carbon paper, no. Does the thought of sending your novel, uncopyrighted, out into the world frighten you? Then, be frightened, but send your book anyway. Deal with reputable publishers and agents and you'll be all right. Also, be a good sport. Trust people—a little, at least.

Should you bind your manuscript or send loose pages? Generally editors prefer your manuscript unbound but with, of course, the pages numbered (consecutively, 1 to the end, *not* chapter by chapter). What good is a fancy leather binding or even one of cheesecloth? What counts is what you wrote. I ususally ship my scripts in the cardboard box that a ream of bond typing paper comes in. The box makes an excellent shipping carton and is just the right size. What should accompany your manuscript? A box of bonbons, a glowing letter about yourself, snapshots of your honeymoon? Nothing. Make sure that your manuscript contains your name and address in several places: title page, perhaps the last page, and anywhere else you think is nice. That's all. Why send a letter? An editor has enough to read without acquiring a pen pal.

Add, though, on the title page a sentence which tells how he can return the script to you; express collect is the fastest way to handle that melancholy transaction. Don't expect the publisher to shell out cash returning unwanted manuscripts. He'd soon have no money to publish books. Enclose sufficient postage if you want it returned that way. Other than brief instructions on getting the baby home, say nothing. Let your manuscript do the talking. However charming your letter might be, if your book is a bust, the editor can't help you. He doesn't publish charming letters.

Shipping Methods

How to ship your manuscript to the slaughter house? Be practical. Your book might find a good home the first time out or, sad to say, might make a dozen trips before a publisher discovers your genius. So ship the script to market the most economical way, unless you're rich. If you send only a few chapters and the synopsis, check the bundle with the post office. Ask about sending the script by special fourth class manuscript rate, which is less expensive than first class and, at times, travels as fast as first class mail anyway. In any event, the time difference is so little and the cost difference is so much, this rate might appeal to you. Professional writers use it. If you're sending the complete book, you've created a weighty bundle. Then investigate the dollar difference between Railway Express and the U.S. Mail. I have discovered I can *air express* a complete book from Ohio to New York faster and cheaper than I could send the same package first class mail.

If you're in the vicinity of Manhattan where most publishers are, use shoe leather and deliver the script in person. But don't make a production of your visit. Pretend you are the delivery boy, walk in, hand the package to whatever charmer will take it, and exit fast. Don't linger by the water cooler waiting for an editor to read what you wrote—all of it —and come bursting into the reception area, shouting, "Stop that man! He's a genius!" For one thing, most editors don't shout. They're soft-spoken. For another thing, you might get arrested for loitering.

Some publishing houses acknowledge the receipt of unsolicited manuscripts and others don't. Whether they do or not is not too important. If you ship your script by first class U.S. Mail, have the package registered and request a receipt. If you ship your script by Railway Express, you're given a receipt when you give them the package. You can do one thing more if you are a worry wart: enclose in the package a self-addressed stamped postcard addressed to you. Let the message read "Manuscript received. Date:_____." Leave room for a signature, and some thoughtful child in the mail room may send the card back to you, noting the arrival date, and signing the card with a handwriting so illegible you'll realize penmanship is a lost art.

What About Subsidy Publishers?

Where do you send mother's little darling? Well, unless your Uncle Fuddles owns a publishing house you are in the same boat as any other first novelist. There are more publishing houses than are dreamt of in your philsophy—but you have an entree to none. If after unsuccessful tries with a dozen regular book publishers, you are in need of a smile from *somebody,* you might make eyes at what is called the "vanity publisher."

These are publishing houses which will publish your book if *you* pay all of the manufacturing costs. I am certain that some vanity publishers can point to best sellers they published after regular publishers rejected them, but I have also the uneasy feeling that, for every success a vanity publisher can brag about, a lot of non-successes exist. Still, in fairness to such houses, let's say if you have your heart set on having your book published—and no regular house will accept your manuscript—you might consider a vanity publisher. Have a lawyer—your lawyer—handy. And talk with the operators of your local bookstores first. Ask them about publishing houses they deal with.

It does seem to me that if you're going to pay to publish your own book, the simple way is to lug your script to local printers and get bids. See what a number of different printers will charge for manufacturing your book. If the vanity publishers can cut out the middleman, why can't you?

Why don't I care for vanity publishers? Because I like to think I am a realist. If a regular publisher will not invest dollars to publish my book, I can be reasonably certain that no reader will invest dollars to buy a copy. In other words, we as writers invest our souls in our books. Why invest dollars, then, to manufacture books? That's what publishers are for. If they believe the book has merit, they will gamble with their money as we gambled with our souls. Publishers gamble with their own money—not ours. If a regular publisher, who knows more about peddling books than I ever will, won't gamble his dollars on my book, I'm not going to gamble the butter-and-egg money. I don't second-guess plumbers and I'm not about to start second-guessing publishers. So much for vanity publishers.

What of the Regular Publishers?

They are legion. Which is which? Well, if you wrote a magazine article about flower arranging, would you send the article to *Playboy?* No. The flowers that *Playboy* arranges are stunning, but you get the idea. Would you send an article on natural child birth to *Popular Mechanics?* Of course not. You send your magazine article to a magazine that prints similar stuff. The same premise can be applied to book publishers. General publishers might publish everything under the sun, but all are not general publishers. Some publish only religious works, text books, nurse stories, or sex manuals. Why waste your time and the publisher's by sending your book to a house that doesn't publish your kind of novel?

How can you find which publisher is which? Easy as falling off a log. In the supplements to this book you will find a list of publishers who accept novels. For a detailed list of book publishers requirements, check *Writer's Market*. A study of the preferences of publishers will make you an instant authority. If you have written what you think is a paperback, this reference book indicates paperback book publishers. You can't lose. Also, do this. You know what your book is about, don't you? Anyway, let's pretend you do. It might be a historical novel. It might be a passionate love story. It might be a childhood reminiscence. Fine and dandy. Jot down a list of a dozen possible publishers you've found in the sources listed above. Then trot to the library—or local bookstore—and check the recent titles these publishers have issued. If one has published a book like yours, chances are that publisher will be more receptive than the publisher who publishes only historical fare. This is a rule of thumb that can get you into a little trouble, because to manufacture a book takes about nine months. The books on the shelves represent the publisher's thinking nine months before. His thinking might have changed a little, a lot, or not at all, but you have no way to tell. Still, the odds are in your favor. Better to send your lusty novel to a house which has published such prose than to one which publishes only cookbooks.

Okay, so one way or another, you've picked the publishing house that will be blessed with getting first crack at the nation's newest novelist. Don't stop with one publisher. True, you will send your book to only one publisher at a time, but pick a second choice, then a third. And so on. After all, the first publisher might not look upon your book as a blessing. Fie on him! What does *he* know! Still, if he should ship your script back, don't shoot yourself. Don't decry the state of literature in the land. No sour grapes, please. Send your book right back out to the second publisher on your list, and then the third, and on, and on. Keep sending your book out. Some of mine, before they found a home, visited more publishing houses than modesty will allow me to list. But if I had stopped sending the first book out after its first rejection, I'd still be writing advertising copy. A manuscript can't sell unless it is out to market. Editors don't break into houses to steal them.

Do You Need a Lawyer?

Suppose that shining day arrives when the letter from the publisher reads:

". . .enclosed is our standard contract."

What then? Should you run out and hire a lawyer? Well, I have nothing against the legal profession, but unless your lawyer knows something about the publishing world, he is not going to know much more about what's to your advantage than you will. I go on the uncomplicated premise that reputable publishing houses are in business to publish books and not to bilk me. Why publish a writer's novel if, because he's been swindled, he hurries elsewhere as soon as he can? Be a trusting soul. Publishing contracts are pretty much the same. The wording may vary from one contract to another, but generally, all contracts are designed to achieve the same goals: to make the writer *and* the publisher rich. Most of the time this happens to neither, but publishers and writers are dreamers. Don't spoil our fun by being practical.

If you don't have an agent (and we'll get to them in a moment) the contract the publisher offers will say nice things like, should the publisher sell the movie rights to your book, the publisher will collect an agent's fee for this effort which was above and beyond the call of duty. Why quibble? The publisher charges much the same as an agent would. And certainly, the publisher with his contracts is in a better position than you are to make a movie sale. The contract will say the same thing about serial rights, that is, peddling parts of the book to a magazine. Don't worry. Let him act as your agent if you have no agent. The contract will probably ask for first look at your next book, which is fine and dandy, too, isn't it? The publisher is gambling on your first effort. Besides, suddenly you're ahead of the game. When you started out, no one cared, and here you are with a publisher wanting to see a book you haven't even written!

The quibbling areas of the standard contract are, I suppose, the dollar amount of the cash advance and the sliding scale of payment (ten percent on the first x thousand copies sold, twelve and a half percent on the next x thousand, and fifteen percent on all copies thereafter) but relax. You're a new novelist and unknown. You're in no position to quibble and besides, do you want to? The publisher has been in the racket a long time. He estimates his dollar advance to you on the basis of how many books he figures will be sold. Considering the general weakness of the sale of first novels, I would say the publisher estimates the sales generously—in your favor. So don't fuss over the advance because that's all it is: an advance. If your book sells more, you'll get more. If your book sells only enough to earn the advance, you're in trouble. Why rob a publisher for a big advance? You don't want him to rob you. Accept the advance with good grace and don't fuss about the payment scale, either. Later on things might be different, but meanwhile, play life cool.

How Important Is an Agent?

Would a publisher rather do business with an agent or directly with the author? Publishers couldn't care less how the transaction is consummated. Oh, I suppose if the author is an obnoxious oaf with garlic on his breath, a publisher might feel better sitting down with the writer's agent. But in the final analysis, publishers don't care. Whether you do business with your publisher directly or through an agent is no skin off the publisher's nose. He won't be angry if you have an agent. He won't be angry if you don't. And if you think an agent is essential in marketing your book, think again, which brings us to the question, how essential are writers' agents? Simply put, a writer's agent acts as a go-between between you and the publisher. You might need a go-between (is that garlic I detect?) or you might not.

Although I happen to be fond of writers' agents I am not so in love with them that I lose my sense of perspective. A basic truth exists: no agent in his right mind—or any other kind—can sell anything you write if what you write has no value. An agent can deliver (by messenger or the U.S. Mail) your manuscript to an editor; or an agent can, perhaps, pave the way for your manuscript's arrival with a telephone call to an editor. But in the end, your manuscript and not the agent must do the selling. Agents know this. Editors know this. And writers should know this. To have a writer's agent is to have no guarantee your book will sell. You can do exactly as the agent does: send your book to likely publishers. True, your script will end in the "slush pile" (don't let the name frighten you) but chances are even *with* an agent acting as mother hen your script would have ended there. Your efforts will be given an honest reading by a first reader who, although young in the profession, is a sharp cookie. If your story has merit, your writing will be passed along and finally reach the editor's desk. No scripts are ignored. All scripts are read. An agent's name on your script might get you a faster reading (because an agent, in essence, acts as the publishing house's first reader, you see) but at this moment in your career, fast or slow reading is not the issue, is it? Your worry is that someone in the publishing house will even look at what you wrote. So rest easy. With or without an agent, you will get a fair hearing. Why then bother with an agent?

The agent who charges writers can—and does—justify making you pay him. He points out, "You're a new writer, and it will be many moons before I can make any money on you. I'm not in business for my health. Working with your manuscripts means I have less time to work with what a selling writer offers me. So I can't afford to give you the time of day—unless you pay for it." He'll say these things in a more flowery manner but what he says is: send cash or I won't play. He is acting as a literary critic as much as an agent. But why pay for advice you can get for nothing? Don't ship your script to such an agent. Send your script straight to a reputable publisher. If your script has promise but needs work, you'll hear. You might receive only a formal rejection slip. But if you do, send your yarn to the next publisher on your list and the next. Sooner or later a hardpressed editor will either buy your writing or take the time to scribble you a few lines telling why he didn't. What he says will be brief, blunt, but kind—and will have more value than all the comments you can buy from an agent or literary critic who offers "for a price" to read your book.

I sound as if I'm down on agents, but I'm not. The time will come when you *do* need one, but not with your first novel. You will need an agent when your books sell like hotcakes. An agent will be able to get more dollars from the publisher. And then, when that day comes that you and your publishers are childishly glaring at one another, your agent smoothes everyone's ruffled nerves. Also, an agent is better equipped to tell the publisher how great you are because coming from you such praise sounds vain. Coming from an agent, these things—still vain—at least sound reasonable. Agents serve many functions, some sadly beyond the call of duty. They wetnurse successful clients, walk their pooches, and wipe their noses. But you are not yet that successful. Walk your own pooch. Wipe your own nose. When you do become successful, don't worry about finding an agent. A good one—or several—will come looking for you. Agents, as the rest of us do, like to go the way of the winners.

What about second serial rights, foreign markets, and movie sales? If you don't have an agent will you miss this slice of the money pie? No. As I suggested, publishing houses handle these matters, too. Your publisher, who has gambled money on you, is as anxious to make you rich and famous as you are anxious. Some reputable publishing houses are better equipped at these secondary sales than some agents are. The matter of sales depends, once again, upon what you have written. What sells, does *not* depend on whether or not you have an agent. Relax.

Do *I* have an agent? Yes, which I suppose makes a lie of everything I say here about them, but guess again. Each agent-author relationship is different. I don't need an agent who protects me from the bad news of a rejection slip. To be rejected is a fact of life in this business. I'd rather not get rejection slips, but I don't shoot myself when I do. I don't need an agent to act as soothing buffer between an editor and me. I would rather, with or without the agent being present, come to amiable grips with an editor over our problems. I'm a sensitive soul on the inside, but when out in the grownup world, I act grownup. I need no one to make life easy for me. So what *do* I need an agent for? To give me more time to write. Simple as that. Before I became associated with an agent, I used to go to New York every six months or so, waste the time of busy editors who would rather be doing their own jobs, getting from them the "feel" of the markets. I would return pooped, with a week missing from my writing schedule. Now, happily, all is different. My agent keeps tabs on the editors and the markets, steers me this direction, guides me from that direction, and I only go to New York on rare occasions for a quick day. New York is a fine place to visit, but Ohio—to me—is a fine place to write.

So, agreed, sooner or later you might need an agent, but right now is not as late as you think. You're still on your first novel. Wait till that one is published. You won't have to seek out an agent then. That guy at your door won't be the Fuller Brush Man.

So Let's Get Your Book Off To Market

And there it goes—going, going, gone! And there you sit, becalmed. You feel elation. You feel exhaustion. You feel empty. You hate to say that final good-by to Hilda and Herbert. You three have been through so much together. How you feel is up to you. Each time we send a book to market, the feeling of farewell is different. Some of our scripts are raw-boned and husky; others are fragile and frightened. Still, sooner or later we must shove them out of the house to let them do or die. Now, for the first time in a long time, you have nothing to rewrite, nothing to edit, and nothing to do but wait. Well, at least feel good. You have accomplished what you started out to do. You have put one word after another, the best words you could find, and the result is your book, *your* book! You've earned the right to feel good, haven't you?

You've earned the right to feel good, haven't you?

What to do now? Should you spend days, weeks, and months brooding about your first novel's fate—or the fate of any book you write? Why do that? The book is out of your hands. Do yourself a favor. Buy another loose-leaf notebook, fill it with blank pages, and on the first page, write

Chapter One

This will be the start of your next book. You're a writer now. Writers don't vegetate. Writers *write*. You had one book in you. Certainly you have the second—because that is the name of the game. Anyway, you've nothing else to do. Your loneliness will come when mine does: every time I write

the end.

Supplements

What A Novel Is

The novel, like everything else under the sun behind the nuclear cloud, is not what it used to be. What used it to be, and what is it now? We can judge roughly by citing examples—much as one may describe with the hand a spiral in the air to explain a winding staircase—but the examples themselves are apt to seem strange bedfellows. How reliable is a system of classification that lumps under one head *Moby Dick, Madame Bovary, Robinson Crusoe, Huckleberry Finn, The Magic Mountain, Crime and Punishment, Don Quixote, The Trial, Ulysses,* and *The Plague*? What are we to make of an alliance of *Catcher In The Rye, The Once And Future King, Snow White, Catch 22, Hopscotch, God Bless You, Mr. Rosewater,* and *Lord Malquist And Mr. Moon*? Are all these works novels? Yes, certainly. What have they in common? They are all novels. The novel is a genus of snowflakes.

Having taken note of the difficulties, however, we cannot just abandon the defining of a novel if we intend to write one. A tidy definition that will encompass all novels is sure to elude us, but let's try one anyway. A novel is a story of a certain length, furnished with meaning. That's full of holes; it is threadbare, but it may, like an old coat, yet prove serviceable.

E. M. Forster has remarked that "the highest factor common to all novels" is that they "tell a story". Very well, then we can begin with a story. A story is the recital of an event or series of events. Does a story alone then make a novel? No. What is it that causes your attention to wander when your neighbor stops by for a cup of coffee and relates in

the course of other small talk a "story" about the two-week vacation
from which he has just returned? He tells you that he has walked on the
beach with his children and his wife, visited this or that historical mon-
ument, seen two old friends, had a flat tire during the trip home. He has
returned; you are glad (guiltily perhaps) when the narrative comes to an
end. Because, unless your neighbor is an extraordinary narrator, the
"story" has no quality to fix itself in your mind and little quality to entertain. The events are not connected thematically and there has been
no conflict to make a dramatic impression upon your consciousness or
emotions. Your friend's account of his vacation lacks two qualities a
novel must have—conflict and meaning.

Conflict

Conflict, like the novel itself, is probably best described by citing examples. Conflict is a battle of opposing forces. Every good novel has such
a battle. A novel can get by without an old fashioned plot, but it cannot
run without a central conflict.

The value of conflict to a novel may be seen easily enough if we try
to think what would happen to any given story if it were without a conflict. What sort of story would *Madame Bovary* be if Emma Bovary
thought herself too good for her husband and so did her lover and so
did the neighbors and so she went away with her lover and lived gaily
and without remorse for ever more? What if Robinson Crusoe had arrived on that island to find a snug, well-stocked cabin and a ship's
schedule posted on the wall. He would only have had to make himself
comfortable and wait; the boat would have come, and off he would
have gone. Off also would have gone the novel, because the novel is
about his struggle with, his battle to survive in spite of his hostile environment. Suppose the young narrator in *Rebecca* had decided to be
sensible and not marry the older man? She would have gone to
America with her female employer, Maxim would have returned alone
to Manderley. She would never have encounted the conflict with the
influence of the dead Rebecca's evil life, and there would have been no
story. What if Huck had decided that he should count himself lucky

that the Widow Douglas had taken an interest in him and had not run from the strictures of the world she represents? There never would have been that exciting trip down the Mississippi, there never would have been that adventure the child in all of us dreams about, the adventure that is life itself. What if Lord Jim had shrugged off his jumping from the endangered ship? Suppose he had said, "Well, after all, it was a stressful moment. It could have happened to anybody." Had Jim, because of his make-up, never had to wrestle with himself, had he not felt morally bound to battle the guilt of his weakness, there would have been no novel.

In *The Spy Who Came In From The Cold*, Leamas tries hard to struggle out of the coils of his life as a secret agent. He tries desperately simply to be a human being, to be able to love and live with Anne, the quiet librarian who further complicates his already complicated life because she belongs to the Communist party. Both Leamas and Anne are rather dull. Without the conflict against which they strive to be together, there would be no novel. In *The Sun Also Rises*, what would happen without the insanity of the war that keeps the two lovers apart? What about *The Old Man And The Sea*? What would there be about that old man to cause anybody at all to read about him without his fierce conflict with the sea for survival and without the conflict between his pride in his skill and the strength of the big fish? The old man pits himself against his environment for his very life, as we all in some measure must, and we read about him gladly because we care about such a conflict. His life, and the lives of all fictional characters, have meaning for us because we recognize in their struggles against their worlds, against themselves, against their antagonists, against death and destruction, the patterns of meaning we sense in our own encounters with experience.

Meaning

Out of the struggle, the conflict of the novel, comes its meaning, that third element without which a novel is really not much good. Story in a novel implies a working out of events so that their meaning is demonstrated. The events in Emma Bovary's life, without her wretched death, would be no novel at all. Her death is the final expression of the meaning to be found in each of the preceding events in the story: the meaning (theme, if you like) of what ungoverned vanity may do to an otherwise ordinary young woman.

All of the events of a novel ought to add up to some meaning. That is, when we look at all of the events of a novel, we should be able to say something meaningful about them. We need not be able to express the meaning of a novel in a sentence or to render it as a maxim, but something should come out of the relating of all the incidents of the story.

Arthur Hailey, in *Hotel*, his detailed chronicle of the workings, both human and mechanical, of a large luxury hotel, draws some meaning from the institution itself. The important matter in this novel, beyond surface considerations of character and plot, is the stability of the institution, which Hailey sees as beneficent to human beings, if run in a competent manner. The plots and sub-plots in this book are many, but chiefly it is the story of Peter McDermott, general manager of The St. Gregory Hotel in New Orleans. Both McDermott and the hotel face daily problems as well as impending major crises, and the novel concerns both their triumphs over the vagaries of their interconnected fortunes. McDermott is trying to rebuild his career as a hotelman, after a personal disaster which has caused him to be blacklisted by the big hotel chains. The St. Gregory, an independent hotel in the old tradition of careful personal service to the traveler, is in financial difficulties and is in danger of being absorbed by one of the large hotel chains, whose hotels are run efficiently but where the profit motive takes precedence over personal service. Within the small world of *Hotel*, the destinies of McDermott and the institution and its employees and guests are worked out through a series of incidents and disasters. In the end. order and right win out over the evil and disorder of hotel thieves, ill-intentioned hotel guests, deadbeats, incompetents, bigotry, and personal cruelty. The hotel has been bought, not by the chain but by a benevolent and eccentric millionaire who installs Peter as executive vice president, insuring that The St. Gregory will retain its character as a personal service hotel. Beyond what is obvious in the novel, perhaps what Hailey is saying is that an institution like The St. Gregory, whose mission is "to welcome the traveler, sustain him, provide him with rest, and speed him on" represents a kind of beneficial human order which ought by right to endure.

The novel begins in real life, but upon the materials of real life—experience—we have to impose the meaning. We cannot record merely what we have observed. We begin with the events of real life, but we depart at once into imaginative truth. Unless experience is distorted for dramatic inequity, it comes out neutral in tone, meticulously real perhaps, but without emotional impact. So we fracture and distort experience to point out patterns of meaning in the experience.

For instance: Joseph Heller's brilliant novel, *Catch 22*, shows us that wars are organized and run by men who are driven far oftener by motives of personal ambition, petty rivalry, and material gain than by the lofty principles they avow. The events of the novel are wildly comic and have not much actual relationship to the way in which a military organization is run, but they have a truthful correspondence to the meaning of the experience of being forced to kill futilely and senselessly. The main character, Yossarian, is a seasoned fighter pilot in World War II. He has flown many missions for his wing, but he has come to be horrified by his job, by the death and the destruction, and he comes to understand, in the course of the novel, that no matter how many missions he flies, how many times he faces the hideous terrors of killing and being killed, he has always, because of Catch 22 in the rules, to fly one more mission, or twelve more or twenty-two more. Catch 22 is the kicker in the system you can't beat. Yossarian, who has the good sense and good taste to like being alive and who wants only to let everybody else live too, is trapped by the system. There is no final help for Yossarian's plight, which is the plight of us all, but there is a fine kind of provisional triumph for the indomitable human spirit in Yossarian's final escape into life. He finally decides to put aside whatever tenuous notions about honor he has had and opt out of the continuing insanity by deserting. But he cannot escape entirely even so. Always, somewhere around every corner, there lurks a deranged girl with a knife, who blames Yossarian irrationally for the death of her lover, and who has sworn to avenge him. Yossarian does usually manage to be a fraction ahead of the knife when it comes down, and he takes off grimly and merrily and runs for his life. The events at the end are as absurd as at the beginning, but Heller is saying that life is absurd and that you do have to run for it, when confronted with the nihilistic lunacy of the systems devised by the evil in men.

Character

All novels begin—novelists and critics generally agree—in character. The novel idea may not originate with character, but character is the first vehicle for expression to which the author must look after he gets the idea. The novel is, after all, a chronicle of human experience. The operative words here are *human* and *experience.* How interesting a story is is a function of how interesting its personages are.

We enter into the experience of a novel through its characters, by living their experiences. And, in a very real sense, we become what we pretend to be. We learn their bitter lessons, comprehend their meaning, are not only purged emotionally but instructed morally. We are changed. We understand more because we have experienced in the space of the novel a whole life. We profit by the fictional experience almost as much as by having actually had the experience, but without the attendant personal consequences of the real experience. If the novelist is skilled enough in dramatization to make us believe in the reality of the character he is writing about, then the experience is as truly ours as if we had lived it and may be said to have a markedly similar effect upon our subsequent behavior and feeling about life. Perhaps being able to get off scot free, wiser but none the sadder, from our errors, follies, deceptions, blunders, immoralities and weaknesses, is the chief delight of the novel. However they may ultimately affect us, the characters are the chief means by which we express the other important parts of the novel—the story, the conflict, and the meaning.

The Modern Novel

The *modern* novel can be nearly anything. It may be a reminiscence (*Yesterday* by Maria Dermont); it may be an historical fantasy (*The*

Once And Future King by T. H. White); it may be a subtle delineation of the human condition (*Thousand Cranes* by Yasunari Kawabata); a grotesquely protean nightmare (*The Tin Drum* by Gunther Grass); an exercise in the subliminal (*Snow White* by Donald Barthelme); or a wild and intricate game (*Hopscotch* by Julio Cortazar). You can get by well enough without a plot or a conventional chronology so long as you have a conflict and interesting characters and an interesting style. Your characters certainly needn't be paragons of virtue, and your world view needn't be cheerful. Even so, the reading public is hardly sneering even now at the old fashioned novel. The novel used to have a beginning, a middle, and an end—those venerable story qualities still so wistfully honored by some editors; and some modern novels still do. Consider the popularity of *Hotel, Airport, Rosemary's Baby, The Spy Who Came In From The Cold, The Secret of Santa Vittoria, Ship Of Fools, The Leopard, Lolita, Dr. Zhivago, Exodus.*

We begin with real life. We record the events of that experience, and we view it through the eyes of characters. We arrange the experience in a carefully selected sequence to illustrate a certain idea, to follow the pattern of our intended meaning.

Whatever the novel is, it must leave the reader with an expanded awareness about real life, which we can, at best, understand only in occasional illuminating flashes.

How To Get An Idea For Your Novel If You Don't Already Have One

How do you get an idea for your novel? Nancy Hale, in *The Realities Of Fiction*, suggests that ideas for stories begin in feeling—feeling a certain way about a place, an object, an observed situation, a suggestion.

Certainly a writer must sharpen all of his senses so as to be receptive to feeling, because the sources of his ideas are all about him—to be seen, heard, smelled, touched, tasted, and "felt". In the novel we invent a world. Where a writer finds his world is a matter largely determined by his disposition and preoccupations. Many writers begin with an interesting character. Some writers undoubtedly find a world in a stock plot, which they furnish with their own ideas and style. Arthur Hailey, who wrote the best-selling *Airport* and *Hotel*, finds worlds in institutions, which he explores meticulously. Some writers find the germ of a book in an inarticulated rage, a passion to set some matter right, to air a human injustice. Not a few writers say that the inception of a book is like a dream, coming to them in the same unbidden way that a dream comes in the night. Many writers keep notebooks, in which they record snatches of experience, an overheard conversation, a tantalizing bit of street drama, the expression of a stranger's face that hints at hidden passions, the idiosyncrasy of a friend, the look or feel of a certain favorite place, a private musing on what so and so really feels about the kind of life she leads. A writer must come to his everyday experiences with the kind of hypersensitized receptiveness that comes to most other people only when they travel. In another country or another region, ordinary life takes on colors we do not notice at home.

How a writer begins to work the experience which comes to him, the themes which occur to him—in whatever fragmentary or elusive form —is an affair between each writer and his own crotchets. Faulkner once said:

> A writer needs three things, experience, observation, and imagination, any two of which, at times any one of which, can supply the lack of the others. With me, a story usually begins with a single idea or memory or mental picture. The writing of the story is simply a matter of working up to that moment, to explain why it happened or what it caused to follow. A writer is trying to create believable people in credible moving situations in the most moving way he can. Obviously he must use as one of his tools the environment which he knows.

Some books begin in a tantalizing hypothetical question. The author wonders "What if. . .?", as Richard Condon did in developing the idea for *The Manchurian Candidate.*

> I worked backward from the ending, which was "What would have happened if a sniper with a Soviet rifle had shot the nominee for the Presidency of the United States at the convention of 1960? From then on it became a work of literary logistics, of working all of the departments of the novel technically backward, to the very beginning of "Where would such a man have begun if he could have done such a thing?" Then "How could he have been persuaded to do it?" And finally, "If he could have been persuaded to do it, who could have persuaded him?" So it was a matter of understanding American mores, politics, reaction.

The writer, like any artist, begins with whatever he sees around him. He tries various combinations of ideas, looks at experience from new angles, in new lights, and imagines new variations.

All writers who are able to analyze the processes involved in their work emphasize the way in which an idea, once under way, takes over and dictates its own logical working out. Rarely does the story for a novel spring full-blown into a writer's mind. E. B. White says that writing not only drains the mind but supplies it too. And more than one writer, trying to explain his methods, mentions the charming lady who never knew what she thought until she saw what she had said. Alberto Moravia, in talking about the genesis of his *Woman of Rome,* says:

> I never work from notes. I had met a woman of Rome—ten years before. Her life had nothing to do with the novel, but I remembered her, she seemed to set off a spark. . .When I sit down to write;. . .I never know what it's going to be till I'm

under way. I trust in inspiration, which sometimes comes and sometimes doesn't. But I don't sit back waiting for it. I work *every* day.

The point seems to be that any material, however fleetingly it is glimpsed, can be worked into a story. Perhaps you have seen a certain situation which puzzles you. You have observed a single encounter in a restaurant between a man and his wife. The man has been needlessly cruel to his wife over some small matter—say, a dispute over what to order—and has humiliated her. The wife, although embarrassed, seems submissive. That is all there is to the matter as you have seen it. Yet, something in her manner may have suggested to you that she herself provoked the cruelty. From this brief snatch of observed experience, you could easily build a story. Let us say that you are currently interested in the idea that human relationships are not always as simple as they look. Depending upon what point you want to make, you might begin to play with your materials by thinking "Suppose" or "What if. . .?" You might decide that the wife is working out some terrible and devious vengeance upon her husband. Perhaps their only child has died in an accident which is not the fault of the husband, but for which the wife blames him nonetheless. The wife has become outwardly patient and longsuffering in her grief, but entices her husband into petty cruelties to prove to the world that he is guilty. The man knows that he is being cruel, but she is more clever than he. She can *make* him cruel at *her* will, and he cannot outmanuever her. She controls him. Like an irritated animal, his only possible reaction is in blind, brutish repression. The *fault* is in her taking of mindless vengeance. Thus, you begin with a "feeling" about something, and you work through the feeling until your imagination yields some form, some story which approximates the feeling and demonstrates the meaning it has suggested to you.

Simenon, who created the famous and popular detective, Maigret, as well as wrote a number of more serious psychological novels, starts his novel-making process in an orderly, deliberate way.

Unconsciously, I probably always have two or three, not novels, not ideas about novels, but themes in my mind. I never even think that they might serve for a novel; more exactly, they are the things about which I worry. Two days before I start writing a novel I consciously take up one of those ideas. But even before I consciously take it up I first find some atmosphere. Today there is a little sunshine here. I might remember such and such a spring, maybe in some small Italian town, or some place in the French provinces or in Arizona, I don't know, and then, little by little, a small world will come into my mind, with a few characters. Those characters will be taken partly from people I have known and partly from pure imagination—you know, it's a complex of both. And then the idea I had before will come and stick around them. They will have the same problem I have in my mind myself. And the problem—with those people—will give me the novel. . .I have such a man, such a woman, in such surroundings. What can happen to them to oblige them to go to their limit? That's the question. It will sometimes be a very simple incident, anything which will change their lives. Then I write my novel chapter by chapter.

Or, consider the experience of another novelist, John Fowles, who wrote *The Collector.*

> The novel I am writing at the moment. . .is set about a hundred years back. . .It started four or five months ago as a visual image. A woman stands at the end of a deserted quay and stares out to sea. That was all. This image rose in my mind one morning when I was still in bed half asleep. It corresponded to no actual incident in my life. . .that I can recall, though I have for years collected obscure books and forgotten prints, all sorts of flotsam and jetsam from the last two or three centuries, relics of past lives. . . [These images] float into my mind very often. . .Once the seed germinates, reason and knowledge, culture and all the rest, have to start to grow it. You cannot create a world by hot instinct, but only by cold experience.

From the stream of experience that drifts by us all, random bits stick like poplar down in the writer's consciousness. As randomly too as a wind blown seed, some bits grow, whether the writer wills it or no. Robert Crichton, who wrote *The Secret Of Santa Vittoria,* actively resisted at first the lure of the idea for that novel.

> In the. . .spring of 1962. . .a magazine publisher named Henry Steeger came back from a lunch he had with some Italian wine growers and told me the story of a small Italian hill town where the people had hidden 1,000,000 bottles of wine from the Germans and how they managed to keep their enormous secret.
>
> "Someone should write that," Mr. Steeger said. "It has the quality of legend and yet it happened in our time."
>
> I could recognize that much. I was astonished in fact that this fat plum of a story, swelling with possibilities, was still unplucked. . .Against my will the story preyed upon me, fermenting in my doughy spirit, fizzing there like a cake of yeast in a wine vat.
>
> I woke one morning in March, there was snow and thunder in the morning, very rare and very strange, with the line, "In dreams begin responsibilities" running in my mind. It is a line from Yeats. . .This morning the line was very clear to me: If you dream about something all the time, you have a responsibility to do some-

thing about it. I began going around New York trying to raise enough money to take me to Italy.

Stories are in everything. The writer, slogging through the long grass of his daily experiences, occasionally starts a covy of ideas, which rise like startled birds from the grasses. Their flight is swift, and he is lucky if his mind retains its glimpse long enough to communicate the glory of their sudden flight. These glimpses of meaning, these feelings about a place or a situation or a glance or a gesture, when communicated properly, are precisely what we remember longest from a good novel. They come to represent in some way the quality of the entire novel for us. In *Oliver Twist*, we remember the starveling Oliver asking timidly for a second bowl of gruel and the utter and genuine astonishment of the evil keepers of the workhouse at his audacity. We remember the dream-like forest and the strange lights on the bird-girl's hair from *Green Mansions*; Madame Bovary "clutching the horrible piece of paper that rattled in her hand like a sheet of tin"—the letter of betrayal from her faithless lover; the lowering sense of mystery at the Spouter Inn and the majesty of the sea from *Moby Dick*. We remember Lucky Jim as a house guest, in comically abject terror, trimming with a razor blade the charred edges of a hole he has carelessly burned in his bedsheet with a cigarette, in the wildly imbecilic hope that his hostess will be less likely to notice. We remember the steady competence of the Swede and the calm and order brought to the derelict farm by his quiet skills in *Noon Wine*; and we remember the terrible Spanish twins in *Ship Of Fools* tipping the woebegone, seasick Pug over the side. A novel not only begins in feeling, it ends in feeling, although between the two matters the skill of the writer has caused the feeling to fuse with the meaning.

A Word About Viewpoint

When we read a novel, we enter willingly into its illusion of reality. That's what makes a novel worth reading. We identify with its characters. If, however, we are asked to identify with more than one character at a time, we become impatient, because we can only dream one dream, enter into one illusion, at a time. We cannot sympathize with a boarder who wants to murder his landlady for her sock full of money at the same time that we are—inside the landlady's mind—falling in love with the villainous tenant and sizing him up as a prospective husband. At least we cannot do so in the same scene without so wrenching our emotions that we have to give way to laughter. One viewpoint or the other must predominate until there can be a logical shift—a new scene, or a change in the direction of the intended meaning of a passage. Given enough distance between two different viewpoints—a new scene, usually—we are able to prepare ourselves for the new illusion and take seriously the alternative way of looking at things. We are ready to dream again and explore the mind of the new character and to see experience his way for the sake of the next unit of meaning.

There are four possible ways to handle viewpoint in a novel. You can use (1) a first-person narrative—the "I" of the confessions and personal experience stories; (2) a third-person narrative—in which the author takes the reader inside the mind of a character and shows the events of the novel as seen through the character's eyes; (3) the author-omniscient viewpoint—a method in which the author takes a large overview of all his characters and describes their doings and feelings; or (4) a combination of these methods. Most novels use the combination method, because it is perfectly convenient to do so in an extended form and because to be able to offer a number of different viewpoints is useful to the novelist's purposes in exploring the meanings in his story. A short story requires generally, unless the author is particularly skilled, a single viewpoint for the sake of the story's unity, but the novel *can* admit many, depending always, of course, upon the treatment and purpose of the story.

In the first-person method, a central character involves the reader intimately in the situation and colors the reader's reactions by his own.

> That was the winter I was taken, after a three-year wait, into the coveted Arts & Letters Club, and was able now to lunch at the long table in the baroque dining room with the first wits of the town. It surprised me considerably to find Perkins Godley a member. It surprised me even more to discover that he was treasurer of the club, lived in the clubhouse and frequently sat at the end of the long table in the place of honor. I listened carefully to discover what gifts of subtlety or erudition, hitherto unmarked by me, entitled him to such pre-eminence, but he seemed as banal as ever. Smiling, earnest, with his dry, pleasant, impersonal manner and in the loud voice of the slightly deaf, he would ask the most obvious questions of the most important men. Nothing stopped him. I believe he would have asked Shakespeare if Hamlet had been really mad and Leonardo da Vinci what Mona Lisa was smiling about. And the big men took it like lambs. "I'm glad you asked that question, Perkins," they would say, and then come up, as like as not, with some astonishing new revelation. Indeed, traveling through history with Godley, one might have got a straight answer out of the Delphic Oracle! (Louis Auchincloss, *Tales of Manhattan* [Houghton Mifflin, Boston], p. 85)

Now consider this passage, written in the third person:

> The inconclusive conference in the hotel owner's suite left Peter McDermott in a mood of frustration. Striding away down the fifteenth-floor corridor, as Aloysious Royce closed the suite door behind him, he reflected that his encounters with Warren Trent invariably went the same way. As he had on other occasions, he wished fervently that he could have six months and a free hand to manage the hotel himself. (Arthur Hailey, *Hotel* [New York: Doubleday & Co., Inc., 1965] Bantam edition, New York, p. 80)

We have entered the character's mind. The author has shown us his attitudes and suggested his character; and we have learned at least one possible way of viewing the experience of this particular novel.

Author-omniscient viewpoint employs a method largely descriptive. It is best when most objective—or most seemingly objective. The danger of this method is that characters may seem to be mere puppets, being manipulated by the author. The trick, therefore, is to keep the characters living and breathing, and to allow them lives and attitudes of their own.

> The Piazza della Signoria was aglow with orange light from the burning oil pots that hung from every window and from the top of the crenelated tower. Soderini detached himself from his Council associates in the raised loggia and met Michelangelo at the base of Donatello's Judith. He was dressed in a plain silk shirt against the locked-in heat of the evening, but his expression was one of being coolly pleased with himself. (Irving Stone, *The Agony and the Ecstasy,* [New York: Doubleday & Co., Inc.] Signet edition published by New American Library, New York, p. 377)

The main pitfall of using a combination of all these methods is a too rapid switching from one viewpoint to another. The writer must switch viewpoints only as the logic of the story dictates, and the switch in viewpoint must be clearly made, so that the reader knows definitely that he is now seeing the experience of the novel through another set of eyes. Notice the skill with which the transition from one viewpoint to another is made in this passage:

> He couldn't keep from constantly touching her comb, her rings, everything she wore; sometimes he gave her great full-lipped kisses on the cheek, or a whole series of tiny kisses up her bare arm, from her fingertips to her shoulder; and half amused, half annoyed, she would push him away as one does an importunate child.
> Before her marriage she had thought that she had love within her grasp; but since the happiness which she had expected this love to bring her hadn't come, she supposed she must have been mistaken. And Emma tried to imagine just what was meant, in life, by the words "bliss", "passion", and "rapture"—words that had seemed so beautiful to her in books. (*Madame Bovary*)

She pushes him away, and only *then* does the viewpoint change. We have, in a sense, changed scenes. As with many another matter in the writing of the novel, the idea to be offered and the intent of the passage probably will best dictate the viewpoint to be used, and a novelist is well advised to employ that method which seems most natural to the telling of his story.

Markets* For Novels

Abelard-Schuman, Ltd.
6 W. 57th St.
New York, N. Y. 10019

Ace Books
1120 Avenue of the Americas
New York, N. Y. 10036

Arcadia House
419 Park Ave. S.
New York, N. Y. 10016

The Atlantic Monthly Press
8 Arlington St.
Boston, Mass. 02116

Avon Book Division of
 the Hearst Corporation
959 Eighth Ave.
New York, N. Y. 10019

Augsburg Publishing House
426 S. Fifth Ave.
Minneapolis, Minn. 55415

Ballantine Books, Inc.
101 Fifth Ave.
New York, N. Y. 10003

Bantam Books, Inc.
271 Madison Ave.
New York, N. Y. 10016

A. S. Barnes & Co., Inc.
Forsgate Drive
Cranbury, N. J. 10016

Belmont Books
185 Madison Ave.
New York, N. Y. 10021

Berkley Publishing Corp.
200 Madison Ave.
New York, N. Y. 10016

Thomas Bouregy & Co., Inc.
22 E. 60th St.
New York, N. Y. 10022

George Braziller, Inc.
1 Park Ave.
New York, N. Y. 10016

Broadman Press
217 Ninth Ave. N.
Nashville, Tenn. 37203

*Names and addresses only. Please see *Writer's Market* for detailed editorial requirements.

Capstone Bookpress
6126 W. 64th Ave.
Arvada, Colo. 80002

Citadel Press, Inc.
222 Park Ave. S.
New York, N. Y. 10003

Concordia Publishing House
3558 So. Jefferson Ave.
St. Louis, Mo. 63118

Coward-McCann, Inc.
200 Madison Ave.
New York, N. Y. 10016

Criterion Books, Inc.
6 W. 57th St.
New York, N. Y. 10019

Crown Publishers
419 Park Ave. S.
New York, N. Y. 10016

The John Day Co., Inc.
62 W. 45th St.
New York, N. Y. 10036

The Dial Press, Inc.
750 Third Ave.
New York, N. Y. 10017

Dodd, Mead and Co.
79 Madison Ave.
New York, N. Y. 10016

Doubleday & Co., Inc.
277 Park Ave.
New York, New York 10017

E. P. Dutton & Co., Inc.
201 Park Ave. S.
New York, New York, 10017

William B. Eerdmans Publishing Co.
225 Jefferson, S. E.
Grand Rapids, Mich. 49502

Paul S. Eriksson, Inc.
119 W. 57th St.
New York, N. Y. 10019

M. Evans & Co., Inc.
216 E. 49th St.
New York, N. Y. 10017

Farrar, Straus and Giroux, Inc.
19 Union Square W.
New York, N. Y. 10003

Fawcett Publications, Inc.
67 W. 44th St.
New York, N. Y. 10036

Fleet Press Corp.
156 Fifth Ave.
New York, N. Y. 10010

Follett Publishing Co.
201 N. Wells St.
Chicago, Ill. 60606

Fountainhead Publishers, Inc.
475 Fifth Ave.
New York, N. Y. 10017

Grossman Publishers, Inc.
125A E. 19th St.
New York, N. Y. 10003

Grove Press, Inc.
80 University Place
New York, N. Y. 10003

Harcourt, Brace & World, Inc.
757 Third Ave. at 47th St.
New York, N. Y. 10017

Harper and Row Publishers, Inc.
49 E. 33rd St.
New York, N. Y. 10016

Harris-Wolfe & Co.
235 N. Main St.
Jacksonville, Ill. 62650

Holt, Rinehart and Winston, Inc.
383 Madison Ave.
New York, N. Y. 10017

Houghton Mifflin Co.
2 Park St.
Boston, Mass. 02108

Alfred A. Knopf, Inc.
501 Madison Ave.
New York, N. Y. 10022

Lancer Books, Inc.
1560 Broadway
New York, N. Y. 10036

Lawrence Publishing Co.
617 S. Olive St.
Los Angeles, Calif. 90014

Seymour Lawrence, Inc.
90 Beacon St.
Boston, Mass. 02108

J. B. Lippincott Co.
E. Washington Sq.
Philadelphia, Pa. 19105

Little, Brown and Co.
34 Beacon St.
Boston, Mass. 02106

Liveright Publishing Corp.
386 Park Ave. S.
New York, N. Y. 10016

Robert B. Luce, Inc.
1244 19th St., N. W.
Washington, D. C. 20036

The Macmillan Co.
866 Third Ave.
New York, N. Y. 10022

Macfadden-Bartell Corp.
205 E. 42nd St.
New York, N. Y. 10017

McGraw-Hill Book Company
Trade Division
330 W. 42nd St.
New York, N. Y. 10036

David McKay Co., Inc.
750 Third Ave.
New York, N. Y. 10016

McNally & Loftin
111 E. De la Guerra St.
Box 1316
Santa Barbara, Calif. 93102

Macrae Smith Co.
225 S. 15th St.
Philadelphia, Pa. 19102

Meredith Press
250 Park Ave.
New York, N. Y. 10017

William Morrow & Co.
105 Madison Ave.
New York, N. Y. 10016

New American Library, Inc.
1301 Avenue of the Americas
New York, N. Y. 10019

W. W. Norton & Co., Inc.
55 Fifth Ave.
New York, N. Y. 10003

Paperback Library, Inc.
315 Park Ave. S.
New York, N. Y. 10010

The Pemberton Press
1 Pemberton Parkway
Austin, Texas 78703

Phaedra, Inc.
27 Washington Sq. N.
New York, N. Y. 10011

Pocket Books
Simon & Schuster
630 Fifth Ave.
New York, N. Y. 10020

Bern Porter Books
P. O. Box 17
Rockland, Me. 04841

Clarkson N. Potter, Inc.
419 Park Ave. So.
New York, N. Y. 10016

G. P. Putnam's Sons
200 Madison Ave.
New York, N. Y. 10016

Pyramid Books
444 Madison Ave.
New York, N. Y. 10022

Random House, Inc.
201 E. 50th St.
New York, N. Y. 10022

Red Dust, Inc.
229 E. 81st St.
New York, N. Y. 10028

Henry Regnery Co.
114 W. Illinois St.
Chicago, Ill. 60610

Roy Publishers, Inc.
30 E. 74th St.
New York, N. Y. 10021

The Ryerson Press
299 Queen St. W.
Toronto 2B
Ontario, Canada

Charles Scribner's Sons
597 Fifth Ave.
New York, N. Y. 10017

Sherbourne Press
1640 S. La Cienega Blvd.
Los Angeles, Calif. 90035

Simon and Schuster
Trade Book Division
630 Fifth Ave.
New York, N. Y. 10020

Templegate Publishers
719 E. Adams St.
Springfield, Ill. 62705

The World Publishing Co.
Subsidiary of Times Mirror Co.
2231 West 110th St.
Cleveland, Ohio 44102

The Viking Press, Inc.
625 Madison Ave.
New York, N. Y. 10022

Zondervan Publishing House
1415 Lake Drive, S. E.
Grand Rapids, Mich. 49506

Index

Adverbs, avoiding 119
Agent, writer's 135-137
Aunt Tilly, creating 15-24
Blocking see Plotting
Chapter length 108-110
Characters
  developing 50, 51-54, 59, 72, 92-93, 94,
    96, 146
  methods of creating 3, 17-18
  real people as 19-20
Conflict 142-143
Contrasts, using 44, 52, 53
Copyrights 128
Critics 103
Description
  examples of 43, 44, 48, 49
  limiting 42, 43, 46, 49
  overworked 45-46
  writing 4, 42-49, 58
Dialect, writing 30
Dialogue
  examples of 27, 28, 29, 31, 32, 33, 34,
    53, 94, 95, 110
  making it sound real 27, 28-29
  writing 3, 25-26, 27, 29, 59
Editing 113-125
Emotion, communicating 16
First draft, writing 5, 100-106
Flashbacks 95
Humor
  defining 64, 68
  sense of 64
  using naturally 65, 66, 67
Idea for a novel 148-152
Imagination 52-54
It, avoiding 120
Magazine research 80, 82
Manuscript page, sample 124
Manuscript
  preparing 127, 128
  shipping 128-130
Markets, novel 157-161
Message in your novel 70, 71, 75, 143-146

Newspaper research 77-79
Novel, defining 141, 146-147
Obscenities 121
Opening paragraph 100, 101
Ordinary, avoiding the 51-55
Periodic sentence, using 118
Plotting
  the first chapter 86
  the last chapter 86-87
  the middle chapters 88, 92-99
  the novel as a whole 5, 84, 85, 89
Possessives, using correctly 120, 121
Present participles, avoiding 116-117
Publishers, finding 131-133
Quoting people 80-81
Reader, involving your 71
Real people as characters 19-20
Research
  magazine 80, 82
  method 78-79
  need for 76-78
  newspaper 77-79
Said, using 29, 31-34
Second draft, writing 107-112
Setting
  checking 39-41
  choosing 4, 35-36, 54
  putting a character in 40-41, 42-43
  using those you know 35-36
Sex
  characters in a scene 59, 60
  how much to use 57-58
  suggesting 58, 61-62
  when to use 59, 60
Spelling 122
Standard contract 134
Thesaurus, using for description 22, 47-48
Time span of your novel 92, 93
Time to write, finding 2-3
Very, avoiding 119
Viewpoint 153-156
Yourself, putting in your novel 70-71, 73,
  104